A SCHOOL OF PRAYER AND HOLINESS

Miscellaneous Prayer Exercises

In God's Embrace Ministries

Michael Fonseca, D.Min

ISBN 9781723767463
printed and bound by Kindle Direct Publishing

For more information on this title and other books and
resources available through God's Embrace Ministries, Inc.,
please visit: www.godsembrace.org

GOD'S EMBRACE MINISTRIES,INC.
1601 HIGH HILL ROAD   SCHULENBURG, TX 78956

Phone: (979) 561-8883
Email: info@godsembrace.org

January 27, 2016

Dr. Michael Fonseca
3020 Piano Bridge Road
Schulenburg, TX 78956

Dear Dr. Fonseca,

Recently I have had the pleasure of learning more about *God's Embrace* by our visits, phone conversations and word of mouth. Both Archbishop Bernard Hebda and Bishop Steve Raica of Gaylord, Michigan have utilized *God's Embrace* with very positive results. Like them, I too, have seen similar fruits here in the Diocese of Victoria. Many in our diocese have experienced a retreat or the programs in Catholic Spirituality resulting in a deeper love of the Church, Sacred Scripture and the Holy Spirit.

After speaking with you and learning more about your ministry, I am pleased in joining others and offer my personal endorsement of *God's Embrace* Ministry in the Diocese of Victoria. We are blessed to have at our disposal a program such as this, and I am certain that many will be led to the fullness of our faith and the reality of God's unconditional love for them through *God's Embrace*.

May God continue to bless you and your ministry. Let's keep one another in prayer!

Sincerely,

+ Brendan Cahill

Most Reverend Brendan J. Cahill, S.T.D.
Bishop of Victoria

BJC/ga

TABLE OF CONTENTS

PRAYERS ON COVENANT LIFE: USING LECTIO DIVINA 63
Shepherd Me into your Kingdom, Lord

PRAYERS ON COVENANT LIFE: USING LECTIO DIVINA 83
Make us your Holy Family, Lord

PRAYERS USING THE METHOD OF MEDITATION 96

INTRODUCTORY REMARKS

For many centuries in the history of Christianity, when learning how to read and write was a rare privilege denied to most Christians, many of them entered the Sacred Mysteries and became ardent disciples of Jesus through the vocal prayers that they prayed from memory, and the teachings about the faith that they received from their pastors. Our ingrained skepticism would make us wonder whether such a school of formation in discipleship could really have helped Christians become holy and transformed. In part, our skepticism would spring from the fact that we ourselves have prayed our rote prayers mechanically and with distraction. They did not really help us to enter more deeply into the Sacred Mysteries of Jesus' passion-death-resurrection.

On the other hand, we have many martyrs and saints from among the ranks of the uneducated and illiterate. By the world's standards they might have been insignificant, however, in God's eyes and the eyes of the Church, they were powerful witnesses worthy of our highest admiration and love. Through vocal prayer, their faith was strengthened, and their surrender to God became wholehearted and courageous. Furthermore, we could ponder the reality that each one of our vocal prayers is a sacramental that contains eternal truths revealed to us by God through His Son Jesus, under the power and guidance of the Holy Spirit. Hence, if these prayers were prayed with childlike faith in the transformative power of the Holy Spirit, they would indeed become a school of formation leading inexorably to our transformation.

Our position in this little manual is the following: If you pray your vocal prayers as offered in this booklet with childlike faith, sitting at the feet of your Master Jesus, with the Holy Spirit as your Tutor, the Master's School of Formation will indeed become His School of Transformation. If you pay loving attention to the words of each prayer and reverent attention to the Presence of the Lord within you, you will indeed become a sanctuary where God has made His abode. You will become a citizen of heaven on an earthly sojourn.

Along with various vocal prayers, I have introduced prayer exercises using the methods of prayer that have been advocated by our saints who were great spiritual directors, methods like Lectio Divina or the Benedictine Method of Prayer, Meditation, and Ignatian Contemplation. It is our hope that you will benefit spiritually from using these methods of prayer as well.

There are a few important steps that you will need to adhere to if your vocal prayers are going to transform you. You will need to keep them in mind every time you pray with your own words or with the words of the Psalmist, Church, or saint:

1. When asked by His disciples to teach them how to pray, Jesus taught them the Our Father which is essentially the Prayer of Petition. In His teaching, Jesus laid down four conditions for the Prayer of Petition to become efficacious: pray with faith; persevere in your petitioning; make forgiveness of others your paramount goal at all times; abide in God's will through obedience to His teachings.

2. We are composite beings and need to pray with our whole being: body and soul. We don't pray with our minds alone. Our bodies tell us a great deal about whether we are at home with ourselves or not, and about the presence and absence of God in our lives. You need to be at home with yourself before you can be at home with God. It will help you greatly, therefore, if you make the effort to become still and aware of God's loving presence as you enter your prayer session.

3. The Holy Spirit has been given to us by the Father at the request of Jesus. The Holy Spirit is our Advocate. He re-creates us in Jesus' image by revealing the truths in His teachings. Begin every prayer session invoking the Holy Spirit. It is the first prayer in the manual.

May this manual bring you into God's Embrace leading you into His Divine Trinitarian heart!

PRAYER TO THE HOLY SPIRIT

Summary: This prayer highlights the special place and function of the Holy Spirit in our lives as disciples of Jesus. In His Great Discourse, Jesus gives us a vivid description of the Holy Spirit's function. The Holy Spirit comes to those who invite Him, who are willing to accept Jesus as Lord and Savior. Very deliberately, we ask the Holy Spirit to come and rule in our hearts as our Guardian. We ask the Holy Spirit to overshadow us with His gentle wisdom and power. Whenever the temple was consecrated, in Exodus 40:34 and 1Kings 8:10, the presence of God overshadowed it. Through the power of the Holy Spirit, we will be made into temples of the Blessed Trinity. Jesus said, *"The Spirit of truth, he will guide you to all truth. He will not speak on his own, but he will speak what he hears, and will declare to you the things that are coming"* (John 16:13). We ask the Holy Spirit to purify our minds and hearts so that we will live according to the teachings of Jesus. We can only know the Person of Jesus through accepting His teachings. With gratitude and joy, we state the amazing truth that the Holy Spirit is the Guardian of our souls. He is our Advocate and we firmly believe that He will bring us into God's heart. We ask for the blessing and grace to be docile and submissive to His wisdom and guidance, as Mary was in her submission to the Holy Spirit, so that our lives may be a sweet-smelling offering in God's sight. And we pray in Jesus' name.

(Let this be your Opening Prayer at the very beginning of your day upon rising, before every important task, and before every session of prayer.)

Come, Holy Spirit, and overshadow me with your gentle wisdom and power as I endeavor to sit at the feet of Jesus during this period of prayer. Purify my mind and heart as I seek to make the teachings of Jesus my priority in life, thinking, speaking, and doing as He desires. You are the Keeper of my soul, leading me into God's heart. May I be docile and submissive to your wisdom and guidance, and may my life be a pleasing offering in your sight, through Christ our Lord. Amen.

Reflection: When you invoke the guidance and direction of the Holy Spirit throughout the day, you will experience Him as the Keeper of our soul. Through the Holy Spirit you will come to know Jesus more intimately, and the Father through Him. In living under the guidance and direction of the Holy Spirit, you will become a credible witness for the Kingdom of God! And you will find yourself being re-created in the image and likeness of Jesus!

PRAYING OUR VOCAL PRAYERS

EXERCISE ONE: THE SIGN OF THE CROSS

Summary: We participate in three amazing truths when we sign ourselves with the cross. Firstly, we acknowledge that Jesus was sent by the Father or descended from heaven (the forehead) down to earth (top of the stomach), to deliver us from the kingdom of Satan and sin (left shoulder), to the Kingdom of God (right shoulder), through His sacrifice on the Cross. Secondly, through Jesus' death on the cross, we have entered the life and love of the Blessed Trinity, claiming the Father and the Holy Spirit as ours, along with Jesus who has made our participation in the divine life possible through His death on the cross. This insertion into God's life began when we were baptized in the name of the Father, the Son, and the Holy Spirit. We can only claim God as our own when we have surrendered ourselves to Him. God is ours because we are His. Thirdly, in signing ourselves with the cross, we are committing to carrying our cross daily as we live in the saving mystery of Christ's crucifixion-death-burial-resurrection. We pledge to live in reparation for our sins and the sins of the world, treating everybody as Jesus would, committed every moment to being perfect and merciful as the Father, through Jesus and in the power of the Holy Spirit. The Cross was the ultimate sign of degradation and a symbol of capital punishment in Roman times. Through His death on the cross, Jesus made it the ultimate sign of triumph over Satan and sin, of grace and entrance into God's love and life!

Session: 3-minute Duration:
In the name of the Father, and of the Son, and of the Holy Spirit. Amen.

First Round: Make the Sign of the Cross very slowly, over 60 seconds, as you participate in the Passover/Exodus from darkness and sin to salvation and new life in the Blessed Trinity through Jesus' sacrifice on the cross.

Second Round: Make the Sign of the Cross very slowly, over 60 seconds, as you claim God as your own because you share in the divine nature (2Peter 1:4) and are committing your life to Him in total obedience. This is the only authentic way to take God's name. Every other way is taking God's name in vain and sinning against the 2nd Commandment.

Third Round: Make the Sign of the Cross very slowly, over 60 seconds, as you commit yourself to carrying your cross daily: you will suffer gladly as you eradicate sin in your life through prayer, penance, self-control, and good works. You will suffer daily in doing reparation for others, treating them as you would Jesus, and loving them even though they treat you harshly and unfairly.

Reflection: Through the Sign of the Cross we express the most fundamental truths of our Christian faith: our belief in the Blessed Trinity – Father, Son, and Holy Spirit, and our salvation through the sacrifice of Jesus, the Incarnate Word, on the cross. It is a creedal statement, a vow to defend our beliefs even if it meant dying for Jesus. Around 200 A.D., the Church Father Tertullian wrote: "We Christians wear out our foreheads with the sign of the cross." Pope Innocent III (1198-1216) explained that the sign of the cross was made with three fingers, as it was done with the invocation of the Blessed Trinity. St. John Vianney reiterated a main teaching of the early Church Fathers when he maintained that Satan and all hell quakes when we sign ourselves with the cross. Ponder on Revelation 14:1: *"...There was the Lamb standing on Mount Zion, and with him a hundred and forty-four thousand who had his name and his Father's name written on their foreheads."*

EXERCISE TWO: THE ACT OF FAITH

Summary: The Act of Faith is a creedal statement. In saying it with deliberate purpose, we profess our belief in the Blessed Trinity: one God in three divine Persons. We believe that Jesus is the Son of God who became our incarnate Savior, and as our Lord will come to judge the living and the dead. We also believe that the Magisterium (Teaching Authority) of the Church has been divinely ordained. Therefore, God cannot and will not deceive us when we accept wholeheartedly the teachings of the Church. To believe is to surrender to the Father through Jesus in the power of the Holy Spirit. Through our surrender to God, we promise to live in obedience to Jesus and His teachings as interpreted by His Church.

Session: 2-minute Duration: Pray the Act of Faith very slowly, over 60 seconds, meaning every word you say, because in doing so you are pledging to even die to uphold these truths. It is a prayer that can only be done through Jesus in the saving power of the Holy Spirit who will re-create us in the image and likeness of Jesus:

O my God, I firmly believe that you are one God in three divine Persons, Father, Son, and Holy Spirit. I believe that your divine Son became man and died for our sins, and that He will come to judge the living and

the dead. I believe these and all the truths which the holy Catholic Church teaches because in revealing them you can neither deceive nor be deceived. Amen.

Reflection: Many who begin their day with the Sign of the Cross followed by the Acts of Faith, Hope, Charity, and Morning Offering, have noticed a deepening of their faith in the Blessed Trinity, a greater understanding and commitment to their relationship with God, and an increased desire to witness to the world that Jesus is Lord and Savior.

EXERCISE THREE: THE ACT OF HOPE

Summary: The Act of Hope is a creedal statement as well. We trust God who is everlastingly trustworthy and reliable. God has made promises to us that He continues to fulfill through His Son and in the power of His Holy Spirit. Therefore, we can confidently hope for forgiveness of sin, the help of God's sanctifying presence with us, and sharing in His eternal life. Our hopes will be fulfilled through Jesus who is our Savior and Lord.

Session: 2-minute Duration: Pray the Act of Hope very slowly, over 60 seconds, meaning every word you say, because in doing so you are pledging your total dependence and reliance on the Blessed Trinity. Such total trust and dependence is possible because through Jesus we have been brought into covenant union with the Blessed Trinity with our wholehearted consent and commitment:

O my God, relying on your almighty power and infinite mercy and promises, I hope to obtain pardon of my sins, the help of your grace, and life everlasting through the merits of Jesus Christ, my Lord and Redeemer. Amen.

Reflection: Many who begin their day with the Sign of the Cross followed by the Acts of Faith, Hope, Charity, and Morning Offering, have noticed a deepening of their faith in the Blessed Trinity, a greater understanding and commitment to their relationship with God, and an increased enthusiasm to witness to the world that Jesus is Lord and Savior.

EXERCISE FOUR: THE ACT OF CHARITY

Summary: The Act of Charity is a covenant statement in that we are pledging our undying commitment to God as the center of our lives. We can pledge our lives to God because in the first place the Father has shared everything of His divine life with us through His Son and in the power of His Holy Spirit. We are pledging, equally importantly, our undying commitment to loving our neighbor as God loves us. At heart in our relationships with humans is the issue of forgiveness. We are committing ourselves to repentance for our wrongful acts and forgiveness of others who have offended us. Such total commitment is possible because we believe that what is impossible for us will be made possible by the Holy Spirit. Hence, the Act of Charity is a creedal statement as well.

Session: 2-minute Duration: Pray the Act of Charity very slowly, over 60 seconds, meaning every word you say, because you are offering yourself to God as a covenant partner, making God and His covenant family the center of your life and service. Such uncompromising action is possible because Jesus has brought us into covenant union with the Blessed Trinity, with our wholehearted consent and commitment:

O my God, I love you above all things with my whole heart and soul because you are all good and worthy of all my love. I love my neighbor as myself for the love of you. I forgive all who have injured me and ask pardon of all whom I have injured. Amen.

Reflection: Many who begin their day with the Sign of the Cross followed by the Acts of Faith, Hope, Charity, and Morning Offering, have noticed a deepening of their faith in the Blessed Trinity, a greater understanding and commitment to their relationship with God, and an increased enthusiasm to witness to the world that Jesus is Lord and Savior.

EXERCISE FIVE: THE ACT OF CONTRITION

Summary: Jesus, as our Lord and Savior, is the very foundation of our discipleship. In Him, we are built on rock; outside of Him, we are built on sand. Repentance or a turning away from sin toward God, and an honest commitment to the teachings of Jesus are the pillars on which our relationship with Jesus stands. The Act of Contrition highlights these two pillars of discipleship: a serious turning away from sin, and a sincere turning toward God for help and strength. Sincere repentance leads to a serious commitment to the teachings of Jesus leading to amending one's life.

Session: 2-minute Duration:

Pray the Act of Contrition very slowly, over 60 seconds, meaning every word you say, because in doing so you are offering yourself to God as a repentant sinner who is committed to becoming a holy covenant partner, making God and His covenant family the center of your life and service. Such uncompromising action is possible because Jesus has brought us into covenant union with the Blessed Trinity, with our wholehearted consent and commitment:

O my God, I am heartily sorry for having offended You and I detest all my sins, because I dread the loss of heaven and the pains of hell, but most of all because they offend You, my God, who are all good and deserving of all my love. I firmly resolve, with the help of your grace, to confess my sins, to do penance and to amend my life. Amen.

Reflection: Many who end their day with the Sign of the Cross followed by the Act of Contrition, have noticed a deepening of their faith in the Blessed Trinity, a greater understanding and commitment to their relationship with God, and an increased enthusiasm to witness to the world that Jesus is Lord and Savior.

EXERCISE SIX: THE MORNING OFFERING

Summary: *The Morning Offering* is a daily renewal of one's life and purpose as a disciple of Jesus Christ. It is a daily renewal of one's vows, highlighting the disciple's commitment to covenant union with God and His covenant family. We make our prayer to Jesus who as our Intercessor before the Father, brings down the continual Outpouring of the Holy Spirit upon us and His covenant family. Our prayer is a participation in Jesus' prayer to the Father made through His Sacrifice on the Cross. Jesus intercedes for us as the Lamb who was slain. In offering our prayers, works, joys and sufferings of the day, we are offering ourselves, without reservation. We can do this because our offering of self is made in union with Jesus' sacrifice on the cross which we celebrate in the holy sacrifice of the Mass throughout the world. Mary and the whole heavenly hosts are participating continually in the Sacred Mysteries of Jesus' redemptive sacrifice on the cross. Mary plays a central role in this supreme act of her Son's continual intercession on our behalf. She is the Queen Mother of God's covenant family. Jesus has entrusted us to her loving care and protection. Mary thinks, acts, and lives in Jesus. We therefore offer our prayer through her immaculate heart.

As disciples, our lives are centered in Jesus. We live to fulfil His intentions: the salvation of the world, reparation for our sins and the sins of others, and the reunion of all Christians. Like St. Paul, we make up for the sufferings of Christ in His body. And we dedicate our lives for the reunion of all Christians in the one Catholic Church that Jesus founded. As a further expression of Jesus' intercession, we pray for His Body, the Church: the intentions of our bishops, of all apostles of prayer, and in particular, for the intentions recommended by our Holy Father.

O Jesus, through the immaculate heart of Mary, I offer you my prayers, works, joys, and sufferings of this day in union with the holy sacrifice of the Mass throughout the world. I offer them for all the intentions of your Sacred Heart: the salvation of souls, reparation for sin, the reunion of all Christians. I offer them for the intentions of our bishops and of all the apostles of prayer, and in particular for those recommended by our Holy Father this month. Amen.

Reflection: Many who begin their day with the Sign of the Cross followed by the Acts of Faith, Hope, Charity, and the Morning Offering, have noticed a deepening of their faith in the Blessed Trinity, a greater understanding and commitment to their relationship with God, and an increased enthusiasm to witness to the world that Jesus is Lord and Savior.

EXERCISE SEVEN: THE OUR FATHER

Summary: Just as the Ten Commandments can be viewed as the Mosaic Covenant's betrothal statement between God and His people, in the same way, the *Our Father* can be seen as the quintessential expression of the New and Everlasting Covenant in Jesus. In the Old Testament, God dwelled among His people in the

Temple. He was Emmanuel to them, yet they held God with great reverence and would address Him using pseudonyms. They were acutely aware of God's everlasting mercy, yet they held God at a distance. They preferred intermediaries, like Moses and the prophets, between God and them.

A sea change occurs with Jesus. He brings us into the depths of His intimacy with God by asking us to share in His filial relationship with His Father. His Father becomes Our Father. Through Jesus, God claims us as His sons and daughters, and we claim Him as Our Father. Through Jesus, we have become insiders to God's life, living with Him and in Him as His sons and daughters. In the Lord's Prayer, therefore, we address the Father with the same sentiments that Jesus has toward Him. We address God by Jesus' name for Him. He is our Father and we share in Jesus' Sonship. Consequently, like Jesus we pledge to make God's name holy by living holy lives for His glory, we commit to the establishment of God's Kingdom in every way possible, and we pledge obedience to the Father's will in the spirit of Jesus' obedience, thus making heaven of earth. Jesus makes possible such a humanly impossible mission through the Holy Spirit. We ask for our daily bread, *epi ousios* in the Greek, the substance or manna from above, who is Jesus. Through Him, we will repent and the Kingdom of God will be at hand. Mindful of our need for repentance, we ask for the forgiveness of our sins and to forgive our trespassers or else our sins will not be forgiven. In Jesus, we have received a hyphenated identity, sinner-saints, in need of forgiveness and continually acting like saints. Finally, we ask that through our own complacency and hardheadedness we might never be led astray.

Session: 3-minute Duration: *[Pray it very slowly, relishing the profound truths revealed by Jesus]*
Our Father, who art in heaven, hallowed be thy name, thy kingdom come, thy will be done on earth as it is in heaven. Give us this day our daily bread and forgive us our trespasses as we forgive those who trespass against us. And lead us not into temptation but deliver us from evil. Amen.

Reflection: Jesus is our Way to the Father. We can only know the Father through Jesus. We cannot really know Jesus without entering into the intimate depths of His relationship with His Father whom He has given to us as Our Father through His death and resurrection. We live our lives within the Father-Son relationship, and the Holy Spirit, the bond of love between the Father and the Son, re-creates us in the image and likeness of Jesus in relationship to His Father. The Lord's Prayer ushers us into this Sacred Mystery of God's Trinitarian Life.

EXERCISE EIGHT: THE GLORY BE

Summary: Two passages from Scripture give us a satisfying glimpse into the glory of God. Isaiah 6:3 makes an intimate connection between the glory of God and His holiness: *"Holy, holy, holy is the LORD of hosts! All the earth is filled with his glory!"* Clearly, God's glory is the visible manifestation of God's holiness. The Psalms continually allude to God's glory as manifested in Creation, expressing praise, adoration, and gratitude for the holiness or Otherness of God. These sentiments clearly point to the Psalmist's awareness of God's holiness and goodness being manifested in creation. God's holiness as manifested in Creation, or His glory, is understood and experienced, but cannot be easily described.

In John 17: 4-5, Jesus says: *"I glorified you on earth by accomplishing the work that you gave me to do. Now glorify me, Father, with you, with the glory that I had with you before the world began."* Jesus is the visible manifestation of God's holiness. As Incarnate Son of God, Jesus accomplished His Father's will perfectly. Jesus is the Father's glory, and in His resurrection, the Father will bestow upon Him the glory that He had and shared with the Father and the Holy Spirit before the world began. Later, in His Priestly Prayer, Jesus says: *"And I have given them the glory you* gave me, so that they may be one, as we are one" (John 17: 22). Through Jesus, we have received a sharing in God's eternal life. Through Jesus, we have been made holy or other than who we could make ourselves. Through Jesus, we can be one as His Body, in the same way as Jesus is one with the Father. Through Jesus, we have seen and become a part of the glory of God. In praying the 'Glory be' we are committing ourselves to becoming holy or the glory of God through the action of the Holy Spirit.

Session: 3-minute Duration:

[Pray it very slowly, relishing with gratitude your sharing in the glory of God]

Glory be to the Father, and to the Son, and to the Holy Spirit. As it was in the beginning, is now, and ever shall be, world without end. Amen.

Reflection: In Jesus, we share God's life as His sons and daughters, and we address Him as Abba, Father. As disciples of Jesus, we are being re-created to share in God's holiness by the Holy Spirit. In this prayer, we ask that our lives as disciples of Jesus will be a visible manifestation of God's holiness or glory.

EXERCISE NINE: THE APOSTLES' CREED

Summary: The Apostles' Creed dates from the early centuries of the church. It is called the Apostles' Creed or Symbol, because it embodies their teachings. The twelve phrases or teachings in the Apostles' Creed come to us from the first and second centuries. It was a summation of various creeds composed by the early bishops for catechumens to ensure the correct understanding and practice of the Christian faith. The *Didache*, a text from the early church, speaks of the creed being used in the Liturgy. Each phrase highlights the teachings of Jesus as echoed by the Apostles under the guidance of the Holy Spirit. This creed is a great gift to us from the early Church.

Session: 5-minute Duration:

[Pray it very slowly, relishing the profound truths of our faith embedded in this ancient apostolic prayer]

I believe in God the Father almighty, Creator of heaven and earth,

and in Jesus Christ, His Son our Lord

who was conceived by the Holy Spirit, was born of the virgin Mary,

suffered under Pontius Pilate, was crucified, died and was buried.

He descended into hell and rose again on the third day.

He ascended into heaven and is seated at the right hand of the Father.

He will come again to judge the living and the dead.

I believe in the Holy Spirit,

the holy Catholic Church, the communion of saints,

the forgiveness of sins,

the resurrection of the body,

and life everlasting. Amen.

Reflection: Our faith in the Blessed Trinity and the truths of God's revealed plan of salvation is greatly strengthened when we pray the Apostles' Creed with serious intent. This prayer connects us to our forebears in the Catholic Faith going back to our Christian roots in the first centuries of Christianity. These truths are eternal and act as a firm foundation to our practice of the Christian faith.

EXERCISE TEN: TAKE AND RECEIVE

Summary: St. Ignatius of Loyola composed this prayer and inserted it in the last exercise of the Thirty-day Retreat or *Spiritual Exercises*: *Contemplation to attain the Love of God.* Through this prayer, the retreatant makes a final and resolute covenant offering of self to

God, in exchange for the total offering of the Father through the gift of His Son Jesus and the guardianship of the Holy Spirit. In offering our liberty to God, we are affirming the fact that Jesus is the Vine and we are the branches. We do not exist outside of Jesus. We have therefore, replaced our liberty and preferences with God's will for our lives. In offering our memory, we are affirming the fact that God has been with us in every circumstance of our lives, even when we were in crisis. We therefore trust that our past has been blessed and forgiven, and we will not entertain resentment, regrets, and guilt about the past. God has indeed forgiven our sins and brought us into His embrace. We offer God our understanding, because God's ways are perfect. Our ways are contaminated by sin. Only God's outlook can free us from the enslavement of our thoughts and memories. In offering our entire will and all we possess, we are stating categorically that we belong to God and not to ourselves. We are committing ourselves to a life of selfless service in union with Jesus who is our Lord and became our servant! We have such boldness because the Holy Spirit makes possible what is otherwise impossible for us. We have God's love and grace, our sharing in God's Trinitarian Life, and that is enough for us!

Session: 2-minute Duration: *[Pray it very slowly, meaning what you say]*
Take Lord and receive, all my liberty, my memory, my understanding and my will. All I have and possess. Thou hast given all to me, to Thee I return all. All is thine, dispose of it entirely according to they will. Give me thy love and thy grace, and that is enough for me. Amen.

Reflection: Every time we pray the words of *Take and Receive,* we are renewing our covenant vows to God, pledging that God is more significant than we are, God is our everything because He became our All, and our lives only make sense in praise and service of Him as His sons and daughters. We are eager to make this offering of ourselves because in the first place, the Blessed Trinity has given themselves to us wholeheartedly and unreservedly.

EXERCISE ELEVEN: ANIMA CHRISTI

Summary: The *Soul of Christ* Prayer was very important to St. Ignatius and acts as a prefatory prayer to *The Spiritual Exercises*, highlighting succinctly the purpose of the retreat: *to enter into covenant union with our Triune God through the Son of God made flesh!* We have entered into covenant union with God through

Jesus becoming man and offering Himself on the Cross as a reparation offering on our behalf. Consequently, we are immersed into the Body, Blood, Soul, and Divinity of our Risen Lord. Our crucified-Risen Lord indwells us and we live within the Body, Blood, Soul, and Divinity of the Risen Jesus in covenant union. The prayer is very graphic on this score. As Colossians 2: 12 puts it, in baptism we have been buried into the death of Christ and have been raised with Him in His resurrection. Along with experiencing salvation as covenant union with the Blessed Trinity, through the Word of God become flesh, St. Ignatius also highlights two other significant aspects of our covenant relationship with God: however powerful Satan might be, the power dwelling within us is far greater than the power dwelling outside us: *From the wicked foe, defend me*! Secondly, while our covenant union with Jesus is personal, it is always experienced within the communion of saints. The last request of the prayer makes this clear: *That with Thy saints I may praise Thee, for ever and ever. Amen.*

Session: 5-minute Duration: *[Pray it very slowly, relishing the profound mystery of Jesus' incarnation, and heaven and earth being joined together in Him]*
Soul of Christ, sanctify me, Body of Christ, save me, Blood of Christ, inebriate me, Water from the side of

Christ, wash me, Passion of Christ, strengthen me, O Good Jesus, hear me, within thy wounds, hide me, permit me not to be separated from thee, from the wicked foe defend me, at the hour of my death, call me, and bid me come to thee, that with thy saints I may praise thee, forever and ever. Amen.

Reflection: This prayer highlights the central truth of Jesus as the Son of God and the Son made flesh: He is our incarnate Lord and Savior. Jesus saves us as God-man! His death on the cross makes Jesus our crucified Savior. His body is broken for us! We are washed white in His blood! We are healed by His stripes (wounds)! Through His death and resurrection, we now share in the divine nature (2Peter 1:4).

EXERCISE TWELVE: PRAYER OF SAINT FRANCIS OF ASSISI

Summary: This prayer has been attributed to St. Francis. Even if the saint did not actually compose this prayer, the words exude the spirit and life of the gentle saint from Assisi. St. Francis has identified himself completely with Jesus. He no longer exists or lives for himself. Who he is and what he does is determined exclusively by His wholehearted service of Jesus and His brothers and sisters for whom He died on the cross. Francis lived like Jesus; he became a servant to all. His blessedness lay in the fact that he became a foot-washer to one and all.

Session: 3-minute Duration: *[Pray it very slowly, meaning what you say]*
Lord, make me an instrument of your peace: where there is hatred, let me sow love; where there is injury, pardon; where there is doubt, faith; where there is despair, hope; where there is darkness, light; where there is sadness, joy. O divine Master, grant that I may not so much seek to be consoled as to console, to be understood as to understand, to be loved as to love. For it is in giving that we receive, it is in pardoning that we are pardoned, and it is in dying that we are born to eternal life. Amen.

Reflection: St. Francis carried his cross daily in his service of everybody whom he met. He was their servant. He endeavored to bring Jesus' love and redemption into every circumstance affected by sin and the human condition, with no regard for himself. Their well-being was His one and only desire. Two key points are worthy of note: the peace of Christ was the basis of all his actions. Peace is the unassailable assurance and conviction that Jesus is victorious over Satan, sin, and permanent death. In giving us His peace, Jesus is assuring us that we can live our lives as He did, always in obedience to His Father, laying down His life continually, day in and day out. Francis was *Alter Christus,* another Christ. Secondly, Saint Francis understood the blessedness of the Beatitudes: In laying down his life, he experienced new life in Jesus, beyond all compare.

EXERCISE THIRTEEN: THE JESUS PRAYER

Summary: To know the Jesus Prayer tradition, a wonderful source would be *The Way of a Pilgrim,* by an anonymous Russian author. The Jesus Prayer is the constant recitation of the prayer, *"Lord, Jesus Christ, have mercy on me, a sinner."* The longer version is, *"Lord Jesus Christ, Son of the Living God, have mercy on me, a sinner."* Various individuals in need of healing uttered this prayer-exclamation, in one form or another. The most prominent is the blind Bartimaeus in Mark 10: 47: *"Jesus, Son of David, have mercy on me."* In the Parable of the Pharisee and Tax Collector in Luke 18, the Tax Collector utters a similar prayer, *"O God, be merciful to me, a sinner."* This prayer captures the very heart of Christian discipleship, namely, that salvation comes from God and can never be something that we merit through our own efforts. Salvation can only be a gift. It is offered when we repent of our sins and turn to Jesus as our Savior and Lord.

There are three simple steps to follow:

1. Locate Jesus' Presence in your heart.
2. Recite the prayer with loving attention to the words and the Presence of Jesus.
3. Recite the prayer to the accompaniment of your breathing, praying the first half as you breathe in, and the second half as you breathe out. Use the third step only when you are seated.

Session: 10-minute Duration: *[Pray it very slowly, meaning what you say]*
Short Version: *Lord Jesus Christ, have mercy on me, a sinner.*
Long Version: *Lord Jesus Christ, Son of the Living God, have mercy on me, a sinner.*

Reflection: You will grow in this practice in stages. In the beginning it will not be possible to do it throughout the day. A valuable tip is that whenever you remember to say it during the day, to recite it several times in a row. Using Rosary beads for the recitation seems to help some people. If the recitation distracts you from the task at hand, do it during your countless moments of transition during the day, when you move from one task to another. Gradually, you may be able to do it even while you are concentrating on your various duties.

The benefits of the Jesus Prayer are many and beyond measure. As disciples get into the practice of reciting this prayer continually throughout the day, they begin to have a strong sense of God's Presence within them. They recognize that they have become temples of the Blessed Trinity. There is a deep recognition of the Sacred within and outside of them. They belong to God and everything else is to be used for the greater praise and service of this indwelling God. At first, they recite the prayer with their lips. Gradually they recognize that they are praying it in their hearts. An abiding sense of God's Presence and the recitation of the prayer emerge in their consciousness. They might realize that even in their sleep this prayer continues. They will have this sense upon awakening in the middle of the night. This practice creates the mind and heart of Jesus in the disciple. A slow and steady transformation takes place. The disciple wants to follow in the Master's footsteps in every way. There is a strong commitment to choose God and avoid evil. One's awareness moves drastically from focus on self to focus on God and serving others.

EXERCISE FOURTEEN: THE CANTICLE OF ZECHARIAH

Summary: The canticle of Zechariah needs to be read as the culmination of a powerful event of salvation surrounding the birth of John the Baptist who was to be become the forerunner of the Savior. The Church gives this canticle a special place of importance by including it in the *Morning Prayer* of the *Liturgy of the Hours.* The canticle traces the journey of transformation that Zechariah underwent after the angel's announcement of the birth of his son, John the Baptist. Zechariah moved from being unbelieving, to being made mute for nine months. During his nine-month hermitage and retreat, he experienced a wonderful transformation resulting in a profound expression of praise and gratitude to the Almighty.

Luke describes the canticle as a prophetic song and therefore, inspired by the Holy Spirit. The canticle begins with a blessing of praise and then highlights three significant landmarks in the history of salvation: the covenant with David, the covenant with Abraham, and the birth of John the Baptist who as the forerunner of the Messiah will introduce us to the new and everlasting covenant in Jesus. Jesus will be the 'daybreak from on high' (an Old Testament Messianic title) and will fulfill the messianic prophecy made in Isaiah 9:1: *"The people who walked in darkness have* seen a great light; upon those who lived in a land of gloom a light has shone."

Session: 3-minute Duration:
[Pray it very slowly, pausing after every statement, and relishing the truths contained in the prayer]
"Blessed be the Lord, the God of Israel, for he has visited and brought redemption to his people. He has raised up a horn for our salvation within the house of David, his servant, even as he promised through the mouth of his holy prophets from of old; salvation from our enemies and from the hand of all who hate us, to show mercy to our fathers and to be mindful of his holy covenant and of the oath he swore to Abraham our father, and to grant us that, rescued from the hand of enemies, without fear we might worship him in holiness and righteousness before him all our days.

And you, child, will be called prophet of the Most High, for you will go before the Lord to prepare his ways, to give his people knowledge of salvation through the forgiveness of their sins, because of the tender mercy of our God by which the daybreak from on high will visit us to shine on those who sit in darkness and death's shadow, to guide our feet into the path of peace" *(Luke 1:68-79).*

Reflection: The Benedictus is the prayer of a man who moved from the shadow of darkness into the light of day and the path of peace. For years he bore the stigma of being without child, and therefore, without God's favor. In his priestly calling, his situation must have been particularly difficult. His transformation gives us strength and confidence to always trust in God's mercy and love. Buoyed by his hope and gratitude toward God, Zechariah's canticle makes a prophetic announcement. It sets the stage for the establishment of the new and everlasting covenant in Jesus, with his son, John the Baptist, playing a key role as the forerunner of the Messiah.

PRAYERS TO EACH PERSON OF THE BLESSED TRINITY

The Method of Prayer will be Lectio Divina

Lectio Divina or The Benedictine Method of Prayer:
'Lectio Divina' goes back to the early Christian centuries. This ancient practice has been kept alive in the monastic traditions of the Church, especially by the Benedictines. Hence, it is also called 'The Benedictine Method of Prayer.'

The first step is ***to read the Word of God*** which is the passage selected for prayer, and to hear it "with the ear of our hearts," in the words of St. Benedict. This step is done slowly and reverently, gently listening for a word or phrase that is God's word for us this day.

The second step is ***Meditation or Repetition.*** We ponder this morsel or word of God given to us by the Holy Spirit, tasting and relishing it, and allowing it to impact us. The term 'repetition' emphasizes the fact that repeating God's word to us over and over, is strikingly similar in action to chewing the cud: God's word gets digested.

The third step is ***Oratio or Prayer.*** The disciple now addresses God through the Scriptural word or phrase that they have received from reading and listening to the Holy Spirit. Prayer leads to an offering of self, shaped by the living word of God.

If the Scripture is short, you can ponder the same word or phrase of God by following this procedure two or three times. If the passage is long, you can break it up into smaller portions and follow the same procedure for each portion.

When Lectio Divina has been practiced for a long time, the disciple becomes quite familiar with the fourth step which is ***Contemplatio or Contemplation.*** In this step we simply rest in the Presence of the One who has used His living word to invite us into His Loving Embrace. In our Christian tradition, this wordless, quiet communing with God is called contemplation.

Lectio Divina has been used by countless holy men and women through the centuries. It has the uncanny knack of unlocking the precious treasures of God's heart and bringing us into silent communing with Him. It unlocks the treasures of our own hearts as well, making us know ourselves as God does.

Lectio Divina leads to Tasting and Relishing of the Truth: When *Lectio Divina* is done on a regular basis, the beginner starts to embrace the life style of a disciple as they are being re-created by the Holy Spirit who is revealing to them the inner depths of Jesus' teachings.

God's word is indeed a living word, producing eternal life in the disciple by the action of the Holy Spirit.

These intimate visits with God are revealing His love to them and bringing about a change of perspective to their lives since they are putting on the mind and heart of Jesus.

Prayer is no longer an obligation to fulfill. Rather it is an invitation to accept because their relationship with God has become very significant to them.

As the beginner advances into discipleship, the Holy Spirit offers the supplicant much consolation, and the habit of pondering the depths of God's word leads to a very satisfying tasting and relishing of the truth.

EXERCISE ONE: OUR PRAYER TO ABBA, FATHER

Summary: This prayer encapsulates the revelation that the Father has made of Himself, both in the Old Testament and especially through His Son Jesus. Through this prayer, we experience the indescribable love that the Father has for us in Jesus and impels us at the same time to generously offer ourselves to Him through His Son and in the power of His Holy Spirit.

Session: 10-minute Duration:
Do Lectio Divina with each paragraph

Father, I am in your presence, awed by your tender compassion and love for me. In adoration, I acknowledge my total dependence upon you for my life, all that I have and possess.

In praise, I acknowledge you as the Giver of all good gifts to me and the whole world. In thanksgiving, I express my gratitude for your generosity and largesse. You are my God and my All, even when I choose to be willful and rebellious.

I am speechless at your generous decision to create me in your image and likeness, thereby giving me a limitless capacity to participate in your divine nature and enter into covenant union with you.

When we were alienated because of our evil deeds, you reconciled us to yourself through your Son, Jesus, who is our Way back to you. Oh Father, you so loved us that You were willing to crush your Son Jesus, by making His life as a reparation offering on our behalf.

Father, you gaze upon me with the same tender love and intimacy that you have for your Son, Jesus. Through your Son, you have given us the privilege to share in His Son-ship, so that we can now address you as Abba, Father.

You are immensely pleased with your Son's offering of us to you, to be your sons and daughters, to receive the gift of your total Self to us, and to make it possible for us to offer ourselves to you in total surrender and obedience, thus conforming ourselves to your own Son's image and likeness.

Your Son has become my food and drink. I now have life in Him, your Life that He shares with you, Father, and the Holy Spirit. He abides in me, and I in Him. And you, Father, who dwell in Him, now make your abode in me.

And with you and your Son, your Holy Spirit too dwells in my heart, revealing to me the depths of your Being. I praise you, glorify you, and adore you, Father, my God and my All. I offer myself to you, through your Son, Jesus Christ, the Lamb that was slain, thus becoming a pleasing offering in your sight.

Living in your Embrace is your desire for me. I desire that you strengthen my resolve to live in total obedience to your Holy Will. I make this prayer through Christ our Lord. Amen. Triune God, be my all! Triune God, be my all! Triune God, be my all!

Reflection: When addressing God as Our Father, our hearts will always be stirred by the same sentiments that Jesus has toward His Father, as we share in His Sonship. In time, the Father will reveal to us the depths of His own great love for His Son, and through Him of His Holy Spirit. And in Jesus we will understand how deeply the Father loves us through the love that Jesus has for Him.

EXERCISE TWO: OUR PRAYER TO JESUS

Summary: This prayer encapsulates the revelation that Jesus is the Son of God, sent by His Father to redeem the world through His death on the cross. Through this prayer we experience the indescribable love of the Blessed Trinity as manifested to us in the crucifixion-death-resurrection of Jesus who is our Lord and God. Such love impels us to generously offer ourselves to the Father through His Son and in the power of His Holy Spirit.

Session: 10-minute Duration:
Do Lectio Divina with each paragraph

Jesus, I have always known you as Jesus, and your name was revealed to us by your Father. Your name tells us who you are on our behalf: *God is salvation* or *God saves*! You have the perfect credentials to be my Savior, because you are the Son of God, I AM, who shares the same divine essence and nature with the Father and the Holy Spirit.

Through your ignominious death on the cross you became sin so that we might become your righteousness! You became our slave so that we might claim your freedom and have your Father as Our Father! As our High Priest you are now seated at the right hand of Our Father, interceding for us and gathering us around you as your Covenant Family.

With Mary, your Mother, and all the apostles and saints, I believe that you are my Lord and my God. With Thomas the Apostle, I fall on my knees and acclaim you as My Lord and my God! Your resurrection from the dead is the triumphant Amen and fulfillment of all the promises God made from the beginning of time.

In your resurrection, I know that you are Lord and God! In your resurrection, I know that your death on the cross was not the wasted death of a criminal, but rather the death of the Lamb of sacrifice, offered as a perfect oblation on behalf of our sins.

In baptism I was buried with you in your death and rose with you in your resurrection. As my Risen Lord, I know that my repentant heart will always receive your forgiveness of my sins. As my Risen Lord, I know that you have gained access for me into God's divine life and love.

In becoming man, you became the covenant knot between the Blessed Trinity and us. The Blessed Trinity always wanted to bind us in covenant love and union with God. Through your death and resurrection, you sealed this bond once and for all. Your sacrifice on the Cross was the perfect offering on our behalf.

As our High Priest, you have entered into God's Sanctuary once and for all, and we have entered with you. In you, the Father loves us with the same love He has for you. Through you, we have the Holy Spirit as our Advocate and Comforter. He is re-creating us in your divine image and likeness, the first-born from the dead.

I accept you as the Way, the Truth, and the Life. I acknowledge you as the Resurrection and the Life, as the Source and Summit of my life. You will come to judge the living and the dead, and with you, we too will be raised from the dead. I pledge my life to you and ask that you join my offering with yours to the Father. In your Name, I pray. Amen.

Reflection: Jesus is our perfect Savior and Lord. Through His incarnation, He has become our perfect representative, able to make perfect atonement for our sins. The incarnate Savior is able to atone perfectly for us because Jesus is the Son of God. In Him, God, the Original, and His image and likeness are bound together in covenant union and love. Jesus is God's mercy incarnate. Jesus is indeed our Way, Truth, and Life.

EXERCISE THREE: OUR PRAYER TO THE HOLY SPIRIT

Summary: This prayer encapsulates the revelation that the Holy Spirit is the Third Person of the Blessed Trinity sent to us by the Father at the request of Jesus, the Son of God and our Savior. Through this prayer we experience the indescribable love of the Blessed Trinity as manifested for us in the crucifixion-death-resurrection of Jesus who is our Lord and God and the Outpouring of His Holy Spirit upon us. Such love impels us to generously offer ourselves to the Father through His Son in the power of His Holy Spirit.

Session: 10-minute Duration:
Do Lectio Divina with each paragraph

Holy Spirit, I praise and adore you as God, as the Third Person of the Blessed Trinity. You are the Giver of God's Life. You are the divine Breath of my life, the Keeper of my soul. You scrutinize all matters, even the depths of God.

In times past, you spoke through the prophets, preparing God's covenant family for Jesus. In these last days, you speak to us through Jesus, the Word of God, revealing to us the profound truths of His teaching, and re-creating us in His image and likeness. You are the gift of the Father's love, given to us at Jesus' request.

Jesus described you as another Advocate who would dwell among us as Emmanuel. Jesus also told us that you would reveal the inner truths of His teachings. I thank you for revealing Jesus to me, for probing the depths of my being with His compassion and love and strengthening my resolve to be His faithful disciple.

I thank you for revealing the Father to me through Jesus, for experiencing the Father's love for me in the fullness and tenderness of His love for Jesus. I thank you for deepening my relationship with you, for mentoring me in covenant union and life with God.

Jesus said that you would have a forensic role, convicting the world regarding sin and righteousness, and condemning Satan. I thank you for deepening my faith in Jesus as my Savior and Lord. I acknowledge Jesus as my Lord and Savior who sits at the right hand of the Father in glory, interceding on our behalf.

I thank you for convicting the values of the world in me, showing me how deceptive and illusory they are. I thank you for showing me that Satan has been vanquished and condemned through the Risen Lord's victory on the cross. I thank you for giving me dominion over Satan in the name of Jesus.

I have been baptized in the death and resurrection of Jesus. In Jesus' death I have been empowered to conquer sin in my life, to carry my cross on a daily basis with trust and patience. In the resurrection of Jesus, I share in the victory of the Lamb that was slain, and His peace and joy reign in my heart.

As Emmanuel, you now dwell in the depths of my being, as the Keeper of my soul, as my Advocate who is leading me to the Father through Jesus, my Savior and Lord. As the Dweller of my soul, along with the Father and the Son, I am now privileged to be God's abode and your Sanctuary.

I thank you for journeying with me on a daily basis, comforting and strengthening me in my daily trials. I thank you for convicting me when I pay scant heed to your voice, or even ignore it. You then leave me in sadness and dissatisfaction, inviting me back to repentance and obedience to your authority over me.

And while you convict me in my sin, I never feel condemned, because you are the Holy Spirit, incarnating divine love and compassion through Jesus, and with the Father and the Son, deeply committed to my covenant union with the Blessed Trinity.

Come, Holy Spirit, and continue to overshadow me with your gentle wisdom and power. Purify my mind and heart as I seek to make the teachings of Jesus my priority in life, thinking, speaking, and doing as He desires. You are the Keeper of my soul, leading me into God's heart. May my life be a pleasing offering in your sight. Amen!

Reflection: The Holy Spirit is the Keeper of our souls. The Holy Spirit is the Breath of Divine Life. We need to make sure the Holy Spirit is breathing upon us continually. The Holy Spirit will lead us into God's heart and we need to ask Him to keep us docile and submissive.

PRAYERS HONORING MARY, MOTHER OF GOD

EXERCISE ONE: THE HAIL MARY

Summary: The Annunciation of the Lord to Mary captures the essence of who Mary is in God's eyes, in the eyes of her contemporaries, and in our eyes as we celebrate her place in God's plan of salvation. Through the Archangel Gabriel, God expresses His tender love and appreciation of Mary, affirming some fundamental truths of our faith regarding Jesus being the incarnate Son of God and Mary being the Mother of God. We seek her intercession because she is the Mother of God and our mother as well, as at Jesus' request, she continues the mission of being the mother of His covenant family with whom He has become one: He as Head, and the Church as His bride and body. It is fitting therefore that we ask Mary as our Blessed Mother to pray for us sinners, now and at the hour of our death.

Session: 5-minute Duration:
[Pray it very slowly, relishing the truths revealed in this prayer]

Hail Mary, full of grace: The Angel echoes God's sentiments toward Mary. Mary is hailed by the angel rather than the other way around. Clearly, the angel views Mary as being very special and close to God. *Kecharitomene* is the Greek word, used to describe Mary as being full of grace. It is the past participle form, *having been filled with grace,* meaning that Mary was always free of sin in anticipation of Jesus' salvific death on the cross. She is perfectly disposed to be the new Eve!

the Lord is with thee: Mary's docility and obedience to God's will has been perfect. The Lord and Mary have been in constant union with each other. More importantly, God is asking her to go on a momentous and challenging mission for Him: to be the mother of His Son, who then can become the Incarnate Savior of the world. God is assuring Mary that He will always be with her as He was always with anyone whom He sent on a perilous mission, like Moses, Joshua, the Apostles.

Blessed art thou among women, and blessed is the fruit of thy womb, Jesus: These words express the heartfelt admiration and amazement of who Mary is in the eyes of God for Elizabeth. Elizabeth's baby leapt in her womb at the sight of Mary, the ark who held Jesus the covenant in her womb. We make Elizabeth's sentiments our own and with God and the communion of saints we hail Mary's role as the Mother of God.

Holy Mary, Mother of God: In the second half of the prayer, we approach Mary in her relationship to us. She is holy, without stain of sin, sharing in the holiness of

God and therefore being the glory of God. She is holy, other than who we are, as she has been chosen by God to be the mother of the Son of God! She is also our Mother as well, as we are the brothers and sisters of Jesus.

Pray for us sinners, now and at the hour of our death. Amen: It is fitting that we ask Mary, Mother of God, and Queen Mother of the new Kingdom of Israel, the Church, to pray for us sinners moving expectantly and confidently toward sharing in God's holiness, to pray for us both now and especially at the hour of our death. And we offer a resounding yes to all that we have stated by ending with Amen!

Reflection: When we pray our vocal prayers with faith and devotion, the Holy Spirit unlocks God's eternal truths embedded in them. These truths renew our faith and strengthen our discipleship. Vocal Prayer then is a school of formation at the feet of Jesus, our Master, with the Holy Spirit as our Mentor, leading from formation to transformation.

EXERCISE TWO: HAIL HOLY QUEEN

Summary: The author of this prayer, most favored by current scholarship, is Herman Contractus (the Cripple). Blessed Herman the Cripple was an 11th century

Benedictine monk. He was bedridden and a speech impediment made him almost impossible to understand. However, he was a gifted mathematician and astronomer. He eventually became blind and died at the age of 40 in 1054. In his last years, Blessed Herman composed hymns, and his 'Salve Regina,' or 'Hail, Holy Queen,' is his best known. In medieval times, monks and friars sang it at the end of the day. Currently, it concludes the Night Prayer of the Divine Office from Trinity Sunday until Advent. We also pray the Hail Holy Queen at the end of the rosary.

In the prayer, we are addressing Mary as our Queen, our Mother, and the second Eve whose progeny made the perfect atonement on our behalf. She is addressed as Queen: *"a woman clothed with the sun, with the moon under her feet, and on her head a crown of twelve stars"* (Revelation 12:1). She is our Mother, as she has been chosen to be the mother of the Son of God, Jesus who is our brother! Mary is the Queen Mother of the new Kingdom of Israel, the Church, as the Queen in the kingdom of Israel was always the King's mother, the Gebirah or Great Lady! As the new Eve, she will make sure that we are protected and safe, having the same sentiments as her Son, the Good Shepherd: *"even though I walk through the valley of the shadow of death, I will fear no evil, for you are with me; your rod and your staff comfort me"* (Psalm 23: 4). So, when we pray to Our Lady, asking her to intercede for us, we are always praying to her Divine Son through her.

Session: 3-minute Duration:

[Pray it very slowly, relishing the truths contained in the prayer]

Hail, holy Queen, Mother of mercy, hail, our life, our sweetness and our hope. To thee do we cry, poor banished children of Eve: to thee do we send up our sighs, mourning and weeping in this vale of tears. Turn then, most gracious Advocate, thine eyes of mercy toward us, and after this our exile, show unto us the blessed fruit of thy womb, Jesus, O merciful, O loving, O sweet Virgin Mary! Amen.

Reflection: Praying the Hail Holy Queen regularly will bring us into the heart of Mary. We will begin to understand Jesus, and through Him, the Father and the Holy Spirit, in the way Mary does. Like Blessed Herman the Cripple, we will enter Jesus' heart through the heart of His mother!

EXERCISE THREE: MEMORARE
[REMEMBER PRAYER]

Summary: The authorship has been attributed to St. Bernard of Clairvaux from the 12th century, possibly because another priest of the same name, Claude Bernard, used it extensively in his ministry to the poor and prisoners in the 17th century. Many miracles were wrought through Mary's intercession using the *Memorare*. It is a favorite prayer for many Catholics. Mary is addressed as our mother, given to us by Jesus. We address our concerns as her children, having the great security that she will heed our prayer and come to our aid. We echo the same sentiments as in the Hail Mary and Hail Holy Queen prayers. There is no better way to be with Jesus than along with His mother, our mother too!

Session: 3-minute Duration:
[Pray it very slowly, relishing the truths contained in the prayer]

Remember, O most gracious Virgin Mary, that never was it known that anyone who fled to thy protection, implored thy help or sought thy intercession, was left unaided. Inspired with this confidence, I fly unto thee, O Virgin of virgins, my Mother; to thee I come, before thee I stand, sinful and sorrowful; O Mother of the

Word Incarnate, despise not my petitions, but in thy mercy hear and answer me.

Reflection: Praying the *Memorare* with devotion and filial trust in Mary brings about an abiding peace in our hearts. We know that we are in good hands with our Mother. We know that she is interceding on our behalf and the treasures of God's heart are being revealed to us through Jesus.

EXERCISE FOUR: THE ANGELUS

Summary: By the 15th century, the *Angelus* as we know it had become a common practice. The Angelus recalls the visit of the Angel to announce to Mary that she would be the mother of the Son Most High. She would conceive by the Holy Spirit and would be the ark of the Covenant, as the power of the Most High would overshadow her, as God did whenever the Ark of the Covenant was placed in the newly erected temples, in the desert in Exodus 40:34, and 1Kings 8:11. The *Angelus* emphasizes the fundamental truth of our Faith, that Jesus in the incarnate Word of God made flesh, and Mary is the Mother of God because Jesus who is man is most definitely God! He is God-man.

Session: 3-minute Duration:

[Pray it very slowly, relishing the truths contained in the prayer]

The Angel of the Lord declared unto Mary,

And she conceived of the Holy Spirit

Hail Mary...

Behold the handmaid of the Lord.

Be it done unto me according to your Word.

Hail Mary...

And the Word was made flesh,

And He dwelt among us.

Hail Mary...

Pray for us, O holy Mother of God.

That we may be made worthy of the promises of Christ.

Let us pray: Pour forth, we beseech Thee, O Lord, thy grace into our hearts, that we to whom the incarnation of Christ was made known by the message of an angel, may by His passion and cross be brought to the glory of His resurrection. Through the same Christ, our Lord. Amen.

Reflection: Our prayers are sacramentals. When we pray them with devotion and faith, they bring us into the Sacred Mysteries. We enter deeply into God's life and love for us. We are transformed and experience a deep sharing in the holiness or otherness of God.

EXERCISE FIVE: THE REGINA COELI
[QUEEN OF HEAVEN]

Summary: The *Regina Coeli* is one of the Church's most joyful anthems and is prayed in place of the Angelus from Holy Saturday to Pentecost. Through this prayer we enter deeply into the spirit and season of Easter. We rejoice with our Blessed Mother that her Son is risen from the dead after a painful and humiliating crucifixion and death. The *Angelus* celebrates the Incarnation of her Son, and the *Regina Coeli* rejoices in the victory of Jesus' resurrection from the dead. We congratulate our Blessed Mother on her Son's victory over Satan, sin, and permanent death.

Session: 3-minute Duration:
[Pray it very slowly, relishing the truths contained in the prayer]
Queen of heaven rejoice, alleluia.
The Son you merited to bear, alleluia,
Has risen as He said, alleluia.
Pray for us to God, alleluia.
Rejoice and be glad, O Virgin Mary, alleluia.
For the Lord has truly risen, alleluia.
Let us pray: O God, you have given joy to the world by the resurrection of your Son, our Lord Jesus Christ. Through the prayers of His mother, the Virgin Mary,

bring us to the happiness of eternal life. We ask this through Christ our Lord. Amen.

Reflection: In our prayers to Mary we experience deeply the truths of our faith related to her. In praying the *Regina Coeli,* we are invited to enter permanently into the Easter joy and victory of our Risen Lord!

EXERCISE SIX: THE MAGNIFICAT

Summary: *My soul proclaims the greatness of the Lord; my spirit rejoices in God my savior:* Mary's response to Elizabeth's greeting and welcome is captured eloquently in her canticle, known as the Magnificat. Her response gives us an intimate glimpse into the inner recesses of her soul. Mary is overwhelmed with God's amazing love for humans, and the extent to which He will go in His love for us. Consequently, Mary is filled with gratitude as she rejoices *in God my savior.* Her spirit is immersed in the love and sacrifice that God is making on our behalf through His Son, Jesus, who is now her son and Savior!

For he has looked upon his handmaid's lowliness; behold, from now on will all ages call me blessed: In Luke 1: 28, Mary is addressed as *favored one! Kecharitomene* is the Greek word, and it is used as a perfect passive participle. Literally, it would be

60

translated as *having been or have already been graced!* In other words, from the very beginning of Mary's creation in her mother's womb, she was with grace, or without sin! She has two responses to this amazing truth made possible in her by the Holy Spirit: she is filled with humility as she is in awe at God's choice of her to be the mother of His Son! She is indeed *blessed among women and for all ages,* as we pray in the Hail Mary.

His mercy is from age to age to those who fear him: Mary extols God's mercy which is offering us the gift of His own divine life out of pure graciousness on His part! And Jesus is God's mercy incarnate that Mary carries in her womb.

Finally, God's plan of salvation unfolding in the Old Testament is being brought to a resounding finale in Jesus, the Son of the Most High, of whose kingdom there will be no end: *He has helped Israel his servant, remembering his mercy, according to his promise to our fathers, to Abraham and his descendants forever.*

Session: 3-minute Duration:

[Pray it very slowly, pausing after every statement, and relishing the truths contained in the prayer]

My soul proclaims the greatness of the Lord; my spirit rejoices in God my savior. For he has looked upon his handmaid's lowliness; behold, from now on will all

ages call me blessed. The Mighty One has done great things for me, and holy is his name. His mercy is from age to age to those who fear him. He has shown might with his arm, dispersed the arrogant of mind and heart. He has thrown down the rulers from their thrones but lifted up the lowly. The hungry he has filled with good things; the rich he has sent away empty. He has helped Israel his servant, remembering his mercy, according to his promise to our fathers, to Abraham and to his descendants forever *(Luke 1: 47-55)*.

Reflection: The Magnificat can read as the worldview of a disciple, someone who lives only for God and sees God's hand in every circumstance of life. Such was Mary's fiat or attitude of total surrender and trust in God. We can ask our Blessed Mother to intercede for us that her disposition of humility and obedience toward God be ours as well!

PRAYERS TO STRENGTHEN COVENANT LIFE

The Method of Prayer will be Lectio Divina
__Lectio Divina or The Benedictine Method of Prayer:__
'Lectio Divina' goes back to the early Christian centuries. This ancient practice has been kept alive in the monastic traditions of the Church, especially by the Benedictines. Hence, it is also called 'The Benedictine Method of Prayer.'

The first step is *__to read the Word of God__* which is the passage selected for prayer, and to hear it "with the ear of our hearts," in the words of St. Benedict. This step is done slowly and reverently, gently listening for a word or phrase that is God's word for us this day.

The second step is *__Meditation or Repetition.__* We ponder this morsel or word of God given to us by the Holy Spirit, tasting and relishing it, and allowing it to impact us. The term 'repetition' emphasizes the fact that repeating God's word to us over and over, is strikingly similar in action to chewing the cud: God's word gets digested.

The third step is *__Oratio or Prayer.__* The disciple now addresses God through the Scriptural word or phrase that they have received from reading and listening to the Holy Spirit. Prayer leads to an offering of self, shaped by the living word of God.

If the Scripture is short, you can ponder the same word of phrase of God by following this procedure two or three times. If the passage is long, you can break it up into smaller portions and follow the same procedure for each portion.

When Lectio Divina has been practiced for a long time, the disciple becomes quite familiar with the fourth step which is ***Contemplatio or Contemplation.*** In this step we simply rest in the Presence of the One who has used His living word to invite us into His Loving Embrace. In our Christian tradition, this wordless, quiet communing with God is called contemplation.

Lectio Divina has been used by countless holy men and women through the centuries. It has the uncanny knack of unlocking the precious treasures of God's heart and bringing us into silent communing with Him. It unlocks the treasures of our own hearts as well, making us know ourselves as God does.

Lectio Divina leads to Tasting and Relishing of the Truth: When *Lectio Divina* is done on a regular basis, the beginner starts to embrace the life style of a disciple as they are being re-created by the Holy Spirit who is revealing to them the inner depths of Jesus' teachings. God's word is indeed a living word, producing eternal life in the disciple by the action of the Holy Spirit.

These intimate visits with God are revealing His love to them and bringing about a change of perspective to their lives since they are putting on the mind and heart of Jesus.

Prayer is no longer an obligation to fulfill. Rather it is an invitation to accept because their relationship with God has become very significant to them.

As the beginner advances into discipleship, the Holy Spirit offers the supplicant much consolation, and the habit of pondering the depths of God's word leads to a very satisfying tasting and relishing of the truth.

Shepherd Me Into Your Kingdom Lord

EXERCISE ONE:
SPIRITUALITY OF THE KINGDOM OF GOD
(REVELATION ONE, WEEK ONE, DAY ONE, PAGE 11)
Do Lectio Divina with each paragraph
Session: 10-minute Duration
THE BASIS OF A COVENANT RELATIONSHIP:
God's love and compassion for us is the basis of our covenant relationship with Him. To make covenant relationship possible, God created us in His image and likeness. In doing so, God offered us the gift of Himself, giving us a share in His life and relationships in the Blessed Trinity!

God brought us into covenant union with Him through His Son, Jesus Christ. Through Jesus, we offer ourselves to God, wanting to belong to Him, to serve Him as He desires. We ask for the Blessed Trinity to reign in our hearts. We ask to become foot-washers like Jesus. To be a disciple of Jesus is to be like Him!

Jesus knows that we are sinners and such transformation is impossible for us to achieve. There is a reality within us that instinctively rebels against all the good we desire to do. Jesus became our Savior and Lord to make such transformation possible. Through His request, the Father gave us the Holy Spirit who re-creates us in the image of Jesus!

THE PRACTICE OF A COVENANT RELATIONSHIP:

A disciple, then, strives to think, speak, and act like Jesus. A disciple lives for the other, because the other is more significant than self. Jesus reigns in the disciple's heart as Lord and King. The disciple owes total allegiance to their Lord and King.

Being faithful to Jesus' teachings is to think, speak, and act like Jesus. Thinking as Jesus does is a slow process. It involves dying to sin and letting go of our disordered desires and preferences. It means adhering to Jesus' worldview without exception because He is Lord!

There will be many a slip in the disciple's attempts to think, speak, and act like Jesus, because sin lurks in our hearts. However, through sincere repentance and earnest intercession, the Holy Spirit will bring about a holy alignment between Jesus' Life and ours! We will indeed put on the mind and heart of our Savior and Lord!

PRAYER IN A COVENANT RELATIONSHIP:

Total trust in the Blessed Trinity is the basis of a disciple's prayer. The Father so loved the world (rebellious humankind), that He gave us His Son to be our Savior and Lord. The Father and Jesus gifted us with the Holy Spirit to be our Advocate and Transformer.

A disciple prays in the awareness that they are deeply loved by each Person of the Blessed Trinity. The Father gazes upon us as sons and daughters; Jesus gazes upon us, as brothers and sisters bought by His blood; the Holy Spirit gathers and enlivens us as God's covenant family.

We pray to God as the Blessed Trinity. Our prayer is addressed to the Father, through Jesus, our Intercessor, in the power of the Holy Spirit, our Advocate and Mentor. We indeed pray in God's Embrace, Father, Son, and Holy Spirit.

EXERCISE TWO:

SPIRITUALITY OF MIRACLES, SIGNS OF THE KINGDOM

(REVELATION TWO, WEEK ONE, DAY ONE, PAGE 46)

Do Lectio Divina with each paragraph
Session: 10-minute Duration

THE BASIS OF JESUS' MIRACLES:

John tells us that the miracles Jesus worked were signs of the presence of God's Kingdom on earth. Every miracle was a revelation of God's almighty power, compassion, and presence.

Jesus worked miracles in His own name! They were pointing to Him as having almighty power. Through His miracles, Jesus displayed divine compassion. Through His miracles, Jesus demonstrated that He was God. The greatest miracle was His resurrection.

All the beneficiaries experienced Jesus' extraordinary presence among them. Many came to believe that Jesus was Lord, and they worshiped Him and became His disciples. After the Resurrection, the Apostles came to believe that Jesus was God. In reflecting on their time with Him, they saw that all along Jesus was God indeed!

THE PRACTICE OF LIVING AS A MIRACLE:

It is a miracle to have been created in the image and likeness of God! It is a miracle to have been baptized into the death of Christ and raised with the Risen Lord. It is a miracle to receive our Risen Lord and Savior in

Holy Communion. It is a miracle that the Blessed Trinity abides in our hearts.

Consequently, our lives are suffused with the Presence and glory of God. As 1John 1:1 would say, *"What we have heard, what we have seen with our eyes, what we looked upon and touched with our hands concerns the Word of life."* Every aspect of our lives is touched with the love and compassion of Father, Son, and Holy Spirit.

Every person around us is a miracle as they have been created in the image and likeness of God. With countless believers we share the same faith in Jesus and all the many blessings that come with discipleship. Jesus desires that we treat everybody as a miracle of creation and of grace! In covenant fashion, Jesus placed us above Himself!

PRAYER WHEN LIVING AS A MIRACLE:

Adoration, Praise, and Thanksgiving would best express our lives as a miracle. Through Jesus, God has taken away our sin and offered us a share in His righteousness. Such love and magnanimity on God's part, evokes profound adoration, praise, and thanksgiving.

In every circumstance, the victorious Risen Lord is present with us. Jesus is present with us in our sorrows and struggles as He illumines them with the strengthening rays of His resurrection. In every circumstance, we share in the glorious victory of Jesus over Satan, sin, and permanent death.

Paul was deeply aware of his life being a miracle. He praised and thanked God continually in every circumstance. He encouraged his Christian communities to be continually filled with praise and thanksgiving (1Thessalonians 1:2-10). The prayer of adoration, praise, and thanksgiving is the best way to live our lives as a miracle!

EXERCISE THREE:
THE SPIRITUALITY OF THE SERMON ON THE MOUNT
(REVELATION THREE, WEEK ONE, DAY ONE, PAGE 71)
Do Lectio Divina with each paragraph
Session: 10-minute Duration
THE BASIS OF THE SERMON ON THE MOUNT:

The Sermon on the Mount tells us who Jesus is through His words and actions. The words of Jesus are autobiographical statements in which He plumbs the depths of His soul and reveals to us God's magnanimous plan of salvation.

The Sermon on the Mount tells us about covenant love and union in relationships. In doing so, Jesus does two things: He shows us how it is done and asks us to do it. And Jesus makes our generous response to God's covenant love possible through the action and presence of the Holy Spirit.

The Sermon on the Mount brought about a sea-change in the history of the world. The world is no longer the same because of Jesus. This is the Good News that Jesus wants us to accept and live from, and subsequently, witness to the ends of the earth.

THE PRACTICE OF THE SERMON ON THE MOUNT:

In practicing the Sermon on the Mount on a daily basis, the disciple moves from the kingdom of this world into the Kingdom of God. Our chains of bondage are severed, and we know ourselves as the sons and daughters of the living God whom we address as Abba, Father.

We understand that total dependence and trust in God is the only successful formula to living life purposefully and joyfully. In our dependence on God, our strength comes from Him. In our trust in God, our fears are tempered. A trusting person is a peaceful person because God is Emmanuel to them.

The practice of the Sermon on the Mount makes us do the impossible, like forgiving seventy times seven, divorcing ourselves from anger and hate, rejoicing when we are persecuted, loving our enemies as if they were saints, living as saints even though we are sinners.

PRAYER OF THE SERMON ON THE MOUNT:

Thinking, speaking, and acting as Jesus does is only possible through the action of the Holy Spirit. The Holy Spirit sustains and transforms us. Seeking the Holy Spirit's guidance and strength is a must. The prayer of petition becomes the staple diet of a disciple's prayer.

We petition in order to abide in Jesus. To abide in Jesus, we beseech the Holy Spirit throughout the day to help us be faithful to His summons in our heart. When we do well, we thank Jesus. When we are struggling, we petition.

In the spirit of the Lord's Prayer, it behooves us to pray with loving attention to God's Presence and to the words. It is especially important that we pray the Lord's Prayer with loving attention to Our Father and to the words. Jesus Himself gave us the words. Let us do our best to make them our very own.

EXERCISE FOUR:
THE SPIRITUALITY OF THE PARABLES
(REVELATION FOUR, WEEK ONE, DAY ONE, PAGE 101)
   Session: 10-minute Duration
   Do Lectio Divina with each paragraph
THE BASIS OF THE PARABLES:

The parables display the presence of the Kingdom of God. They are not as dramatic as the miracles. A supernatural intervention is not immediately apparent.

For the unbelieving of heart, they are fanciful stories that don't mean much. For the believer, they provide glimpses of the Kingdom of God.

A story has a foregone conclusion: a bad beginning will have a bad end. A parable, on the other hand, defies human logic. No matter the extent of tragedy in the person's life, the ending can always be good, because Jesus is the author of the story. Jesus writes straight on crooked lines. Such is the parable of the Prodigal Son in Luke 15.

A parable teaches us how to maneuver safely through life's perilous labyrinth. A parable offers wisdom from the Holy Spirit, warning us of the dangers inherent in our sinful attitudes, and showing us how to act wisely according to God's will. Such is the Parable of the Sower in Matthew 13.

THE PRACTICE OF THE PARABLES:

God's thinking moves along the lines of a parable. Human thinking moves along the lines of a story. It is necessary to trust God's thinking even when the circumstances of our lives make no sense to us. The Parable of the Wheat and Weeds in Matthew 13 makes this point.

For some, the journey into the heart of God begins with a bang. Paul's conversion is a good example (Acts 9). Generally, the parables teach us that God's way of bringing about our transformation is slow and painstaking. God will bring our story to a wonderful end, surely but slowly. The Parable of the Mustard Seed makes this point.

The parables spell out very clearly the right approach to spirituality. In the wrong approach, salvation depends on the individual's merit. Such is the spirituality of the Pharisee in Luke 18. The Tax Collector is honest with himself. Being righteous is beyond his power. He acknowledges his sin and receives God's forgiveness.

PRAYING WITH THE PARABLES:

Parables tell us not to judge others, as our assumptions and conclusions could be biased and wrong. The spirit of a saint is manifested in deeds, not merely in words. The Parable of the Good Samaritan in Luke 10 is a moving testimony. The Samaritan acted as a saint even toward his enemy!

The repentant sinner can only receive mercy from God, if they are willing to live within the parameters of justice: living in the right order with God and others. There can't be mercy without justice. The Parable of the Unforgiving Servant in Matthew 18 illustrates this unbreakable bond between the Original (God) and the image and likeness (us).

The parables illustrate God's unswerving and magnanimous love for us. God's love for us extends beyond the farthest imaginable horizons. Nothing will ever be too much for God when it comes to our welfare. The Parable of the Lost Sheep in Matthew 18 makes this point.

EXERCISE FIVE:
LIVING IN THE UPPER ROOM
(REVELATION FIVE, WEEK ONE, DAY ONE, PAGE 133)
Do Lectio Divina with each paragraph
Session: 10-minute Duration
THE BASIS OF LIVING IN THE UPPER ROOM:

The hours in the Upper Room are very significant for the disciple. They were the last hours of Jesus before He went to His death on the cross in our stead. During the evening, Jesus revealed the depths of God's Trinitarian heart.

There is a sharp contrast between the dispositions of Jesus and the attitude of His disciples. Jesus is totally focused on accomplishing His mission on earth. He reveals some of the deepest truths of His Divine Heart, and most importantly, institutes the Eucharist so that He can always be present among us in His death and resurrection.

The disciples, on the other hand, are fearful and anxious. They are self-serving as well, arguing as to who among them is greater. It is not yet possible for them to comprehend the depths of the last hours of Jesus' earthly life, let alone respond to Him with earnest generosity as His disciples.

THE PRACTICE OF LIVING IN THE UPPER ROOM:

Jesus is now interceding for us as the Lamb that was slain. He is with His Father and continues to abide among us as Emmanuel, God-with-us. In Jesus, the Upper Room experience is ever-present with us. What Jesus said and did then with His disciples, He continues to do today.

Jesus emphasized several necessary dimensions of covenant living for a disciple. He washed the feet of His disciples, identifying Himself as a non-Jewish slave. He was prepared to do anything for us, so great was His love which He demonstrated the following day at Calvary. Being a foot-washer is a badge of honor for the disciple.

Jesus outlined the role of the Holy Spirit in our lives. Jesus instituted the Eucharist. Jesus prayed for us. His whole life was an intercessory prayer on our behalf. His death and resurrection were His Amen to His intercession. Now, as Risen Lord and slain Lamb, Jesus continues His intercession on our behalf. And we pray in and through Him.

PRAYING IN THE UPPER ROOM:

We can only pray to Jesus as our Savior and Lord if we are willing to adopt His example and teachings in the Upper Room and make them our lifestyle. We pray to Jesus as our Lord and Savior who became our slave so that we might share in God's righteousness.

In our prayer in the spirit of the Upper Room, we encounter the depths of Jesus' love for us. Through the Eucharistic meal, Jesus brought us into covenant union with Him, and through Him, with the Father and the Holy Spirit! Our hearts will always be deeply moved by God becoming Emmanuel through the Eucharist.

In our prayer, we encounter the patience and optimism of Jesus even though He was going to His passion and death by crucifixion. Even after three years, His disciples are not on the same page. Jesus is unperturbed, as it is necessary first for Him to suffer and die and rise from the dead. With His resurrection the world will have changed forever!

EXERCISE SIX:
THE DIVINE EMPTYING
(REVELATION SIX, WEEK ONE, DAY ONE, PAGE 162)
Do Lectio Divina with each paragraph
Session: 10-minute Duration
THE BASIS OF CARRYING THE CROSS DAILY:

Jesus who was always God became man. He emptied Himself of His glory and became one of us, becoming obedient to death, even death on a cross. Thus, He freed us from sin while He bore the brunt of sinful behavior!

Only hardened criminals were subjected to death on a cross. Even though He was God, Jesus was willing to humble himself out of love for us to the point of dying on the cross. Understandably, there were varied reactions to His shameful death on the cross. Apart from John, none of the other disciples were present.

The leaders of the people kept jeering at Him, saying, *"He saved others, let him save himself if he is the chosen one, the Messiah of God"* (Luke 23:35). The soldiers too mocked Him, offering Him sour wine and taunting Him to save Himself if indeed He was the king of the Jews! One of the criminals blasphemed Him.

THE PRACTICE OF CARRYING THE CROSS:

Jesus has asked us to carry our cross daily. The cross symbolizes punishment and rejection and for many it is definitely a sign of contradiction. We want to live without suffering and pain while not eschewing sin.

For those who take Jesus seriously, they understand that carrying our cross daily or bearing insults and rejection in our service of God, leads to true freedom and joy. They understand that the only way to experience the peace and joy of the Risen Lord is through the royal road of the Cross.

The death and resurrection of Jesus are one seamless reality. When one accepts the cross in daily life with love and compassion, one experiences the peace and joy of the Risen Lord!

PRAYING WITH THE CRUCIFIED LORD:

The repentant criminal asked Jesus to remember Him in Paradise. He became convinced that Jesus was His Savior. He repented of his sins and Jesus opened the gates of heaven for him.

After Jesus' death, the centurion came to believe that Jesus was the Son of God (Mark 15: 39). Joseph of Arimathea and Nicodemus made public their hidden discipleship. They defied the ban of according burial rites to a criminal. They gave Jesus a tomb and burial rites because they had come to believe that Jesus indeed was the Son of God.

St. Francis of Assisi made Mount Calvary his place of prayer. He was madly in love with the Crucified Jesus and wanted to identify himself with Him. We make the Sign of the Cross many times daily and have crucifixes in our Churches and homes. There is no greater love than to lay down one's life for one's friends.

EXERCISE SEVEN:
LIVING WITH THE RISEN LORD
(REVELATION SEVEN, WEEK ONE, DAY ONE, PAGE 196)
   Do Lectio Divina with each paragraph
   Session: 10-minute Duration
THE BASIS OF LIVING WITH THE RISEN LORD:

The Resurrection of Jesus is the most significant event in the history of humankind. The Resurrection proclaims that Jesus is Lord God. Jesus is God-man. In Him resides the fullness of deity. Jesus is quintessentially Emmanuel, God dwelling among us in human flesh!

Without the resurrection, Jesus would have been a mere dot on the pages of history. With the resurrection, heaven and earth are aligned. Jesus has altered the course of history profoundly and irrevocably. The age of darkness and sin has been vanquished. We are now living in the Light of the Risen Lord!

The resurrection guarantees our own resurrection (body and soul) from the dead at the end of time. In 1Corinthians 15:13, Paul says, *"If there is no resurrection of the dead, then neither has Christ been raised."* In Jesus, humanity and Divinity were united. In the resurrection, heaven and earth are united. God is Emmanuel, dwelling among us.

THE PRACTICE OF LIVING WITH THE RISEN LORD:

The victory of the Risen Lord is always with us. In our covenant union with Jesus, and through Him with the Father and the Holy Spirit, we have died to sin in His death, and have risen with Him to new life, God's divine life! No other reality compares with the resurrection!

The victory of the Risen Lord is permanent. His peace and joy of the resurrection permeate our whole existence, because we are united with Jesus in covenant. Jesus abides in us and we in Him. Even in our darkest moments, He is with us. He is the silver lining to every dark cloud and crisis in our lives.

As disciples of the Risen Lord, we practice making acts of trust when we are afraid and hesitant. We engage in acts of faith when our minds are buffeted by doubts. We remind ourselves that the Risen Lord has overcome sin and Satan when the evil around us seems to be triumphant.

PRAYING WITH THE RISEN LORD:

When we pray to Jesus, we realize that He is of the Father and of us. As God, Jesus is my Creator and Lord. As man, He is my brother and one of us. As God-man,

Jesus is my kinsman-redeemer. Our redemption through Jesus is perfect because He is the Son of God!

We always pray with confidence and joy. We pray with confidence because the resurrection of Jesus is the ultimate proof that Jesus is God and His sacrifice on the cross brought us forgiveness of sin and union with the Blessed Trinity. We pray with joy, because through Jesus we are children of the Light, and His Father is Our Father!

In prayer we always have the assurance that in Jesus all will be well or all is well. He has overcome every principality and power. We can therefore do all things in Him. More importantly, the Risen Lord, the Lamb that was slain is now our Intercessor before the throne of His Father. Through Jesus, we are members of God's covenant family.

Make Us Your Holy Family Lord

EXERCISE ONE:
FAMILY COVENANT UNION
(REVELATION ONE, WEEK ONE, DAY ONE, PAGE 4)
Do Lectio Divina with each paragraph
Session: 10-minute Duration
THE BASIS OF FAMILY COVENANT UNION:

To make covenant union with Him possible, God created us in the likeness of His divinity. This capacity, built into the very fabric of our beings, is essentially indescribable. The finite and the Infinite, the limited and the Unlimited, the imperfect and the Perfect, come together and become one in covenant union.

God wanted us to share in the love, life, and relationships of the Three Divine Persons, selflessly, joyfully and wholeheartedly. This ineffable truth will always stir us deeply and move us to surrender ourselves as creature to Creator, disciple to Teacher, beloved to the All-Loving Bridegroom.

God desired a similar coming together in covenant union between man and woman. This covenant union between husband and wife would be shaped and modeled by the covenant union God established with us. And through His Holy Spirit, God would make the marital covenant union fruitful and life-giving.

THE PRACTICE OF FAMILY COVENANT UNION:

The practice of family covenant union will require honest and tireless effort on the part of husband and wife. Spousal love and devotion will have to combat selfishness and sin, constantly and consistently. Spouses will have to treat each other as saints, while they struggle with their own sin and disorder.

Through Jesus, we have the power to overcome our sinful nature. Our humanity has been restored to its original holiness through Jesus. We now share in the fullness of the divine Light. The Holy Spirit will make covenant love between spouses possible. Let us invoke the Holy Spirit's guidance constantly.

Each day is filled with immense transformational possibilities for spouses: moving from self-centeredness to selflessness and striving to serve and make spouse and children better godly images. In fulfilling such responsibilities, each spouse will grow in covenant union with God and each other.

PRAYER IN FAMILY COVENANT UNION:

Each spouse needs to have a personal and committed relationship to God: being brought to the Father, through Jesus, His Son and our brother, in the power of the Holy Spirit. Without this daily face to face investment in prayer, family covenant union can never be sustained.

With the foundation of a personal relationship with our Triune God, husband and wife will be motivated to pray as 'one body,' praising and thanking God for the multiple blessings poured out upon them as a covenant family and asking for healing and strength to be dedicated to one another in their marital bond.

Spouses need to be aware that the Father gazes with great tenderness upon them, as their family covenant union is the outflow of God's new and eternal covenant with His covenant family through Jesus. Indeed, the Blessed Trinity is the heart throb of their family covenant union.

EXERCISE TWO:
THE HOLY FAMILY'S COVENANT UNION
(REVELATION TWO, WEEK ONE, DAY ONE, PAGE 41)
Do Lectio Divina with each paragraph
Session: 10-minute Duration
THE BASIS OF COVENANT UNION IN THE HOLY FAMILY:
The Holy Family mirrored the life and covenant relationships of the Blessed Trinity in their daily lives. Mary's attitude toward the announcement of the birth of the Messiah, Son of the Most-High, is one of obedience, self-effacement, and total dedication to God's wishes.

Mary's attitude towards God's designs is to approach them as *'the handmaid of the Lord.'* Instead of being totally absorbed in the life-altering event with the conception of the 'Son of the Most-High' through the Holy Spirit, Mary is selfless. She goes to help her cousin, Elizabeth, who is in the sixth month of her pregnancy.

Joseph's world was turned topsy-turvy when he found out that his betrothed was with child, not his child! After Joseph learns of God's plan of salvation, like Mary, he is totally obedient to God's wishes. He took Mary to be his wife, and named the child, Jesus. In that instant, they became the Holy Family.

PRACTICE OF COVENANT UNION IN THE HOLY FAMILY:

Joseph and Mary traveled to Bethlehem to be enrolled at the census. Mary was in her ninth month and would soon deliver their son. In the midst of their great joy, they knew hardship and inconvenience. They were the 'have-nots' of this world; they accepted their circumstances as God's will for them and were totally obedient.

By being missioned to be the parents of Jesus, Mary and Joseph had to open their lives to unforeseen circumstances and events. During the Presentation, they were reminded in no uncertain terms that they would suffer greatly along with their son: *"and you yourself a sword will pierce"* (Luke 2: 35).

Before Jesus dies, He engages in an amazing act of covenant love. He bequeaths to His mother a special mission, in fact, the continuation of the same mission given to her at the Annunciation: to be the mother of His covenant family, with whom He has become one, and symbolized by John the beloved disciple.

PRAYER OF THE HOLY FAMILY IN COVENANT UNION:

Elizabeth describes Mary as *"most blessed are you among women, and blessed is the fruit of your womb."* Mary described herself as, *"Behold, I am the handmaid of the Lord. May it be done to me according to your word."* In Mary's lifestyle and prayer, we can detect all the attitudes inherent in covenant union with God and family.

Mary expresses her covenant lifestyle in her canticle. Mary is filled with gratitude: *"My soul proclaims the greatness of the Lord; my spirit rejoices in God my Savior."* Mary is aware of God's mercy expressed in His magnanimous plan of salvation: *"His mercy is from age to age to those who fear him."*

During Jesus' final hours, Mary experienced her four of seven sorrows along with her son. Her disposition was the same as her son's: *"Father, forgive them"* (Luke 23: 34). As the mother of God's covenant family, Mary's prayer is intercessory, pleading with God through Jesus for our salvation.

EXERCISE FIVE:
COVENANT UNION IN THE APOSTOLIC FAMILY
(REVELATION THREE, WEEK ONE, DAY ONE, PAGE 77)
Do Lectio Divina with each paragraph
Session: 10-minute Duration
THE BASIS OF COVENANT UNION IN THE APOSTOLIC FAMILY:

"For where your treasure is, there also will your heart be" (Matthew 6: 21). The disciple wants Jesus to be their sole treasure, so that God can own them completely. God has called them by their name and they belong to God. They are grafted on to Jesus. He is the vine and they are His branches.

"If I, therefore, the master and teacher, have washed your feet, you ought to wash one another's feet" (John 13:14). For the disciple, God and others are now placed ahead of them. Being humble has become an essential ingredient of their covenant lifestyle. Such a purpose governs their every decision and activity.

I pray... *"that they may all be one, as you, Father, are in me and I in you, that they also may be in us, that the world may believe that you sent me"* (John 17: 21). God dwells within the disciple's heart which becomes God's dwelling place. The Holy Spirit is truly the Keeper of their souls. The disciple understands that they cannot say that they love God when they hate their neighbor.

PRACTICING COVENANT UNION IN THE APOSTOLIC FAMILY:

"It was not you who chose me, but I who chose you and appointed you to go and bear fruit that will remain, so that whatever you ask the Father in my name he may give you" (John 15: 16). The disciple carries out God's mission. The disciple seeks to offer all the help they can, so that God's reign will be established in human hearts.

"And I consecrate myself for them, so that they also may be consecrated in truth" (John 17: 19). The disciple is a hyphenated identity: Jesus-self. Jesus has consecrated Himself, set Himself apart as our Lamb of sacrifice, and asks that we too would become sacrificial victims, set apart, in the service of God's children.

The disciple learns to have equanimity whether they are praised or criticized. The disciple seeks to give their whole life to God, in faithful and grateful service. The disciple's life is about loving and serving God's people, and not about being loved and respected and fulfilled in return.

PRAYER OF THE APOSTOLIC FAMILY IN COVENANT UNION:

The *Our Father* captures the essence of the covenant union between God and His covenant family. It is the Prayer of the New Covenant, as the Ten Commandments were for the Mosaic Covenant. Through His death and resurrection, Jesus has offered us all the joys and privileges of His filial relationship with His Father. God is now our Father as well.

It behooves us, therefore, to act like Jesus does, in total obedience to His Father. So, we hallow God's name in the way Jesus did (John 17: 11-12); we work tirelessly for the establishment of God's kingdom in our hearts and in the world, in union with and continuation of Jesus' redemption of the world. In becoming one with Jesus, we behave like Him towards His Father.

In the second half of the Lord's Prayer, Jesus is reminding us that we are lost outside of Him. And so, we ask for the unmerited gift of always being in union with Him through receiving our daily bread (the name given to the heavenly manna in the desert) which is His Body and Blood; we ask for the forgiveness of our sins in the same measure we forgive others; and we ask as well that we might always be faithful to our covenant bond with the Blessed Trinity, especially in the hour of death.

EXERCISE FOUR:
COVENANT UNION IN SACRAMENTAL LIFE
(REVELATION FOUR, WEEK ONE, DAY ONE, PAGE 114)
Do Lectio Divina with each paragraph
Session: 10-minute Duration
THE BASIS OF COVENANT UNION IN SACRAMENTAL LIFE:

Through the sacraments, the Church celebrates God's life in the midst of His covenant family. Baptism is the plunging that signifies the catechumen's burial into the death of Christ, from which he/she rises up to new life by resurrection with Jesus, as a "new creature" (Colossians 2: 12).

"Baptism is God's most beautiful and magnificent gift… It is called *gift* because it is conferred on those who bring nothing of their own; *grace* since it is given even to the guilty; *baptism* because sin is buried in the water; *anointing* for it is priestly and royal as are those who are anointed; *enlightenment* because it radiates light; *clothing* since it veils our shame; *bath* because it washes; and *seal* as it is our guard and the sign of God's Lordship" (St. Gregory of Nazianzus, CCC 1216).

"In the Eucharist, Christ gives us the very body which he gave up for us on the cross, the very blood which he "poured out for many for the forgiveness of sins" (Matthew 26: 28) (CCC 1365). In receiving Jesus, we become whom we receive

PRACTICE OF COVENANT UNION IN SACRAMENTAL LIFE:

"Christ instituted the sacrament of Penance for all sinful members of his Church: above all for those who, since Baptism, have fallen into grave sin, and have thus lost their baptismal grace and wounded ecclesial communion… The Fathers of the Church present this sacrament as "the second plank [of salvation] after the shipwreck which is the loss of grace" (CCC 1446).

"It (The Sacrament of Reconciliation) comprises two equally essential elements: the acts of the man who undergoes conversion through the action of the Holy Spirit: namely, contrition, confession, and satisfaction; on the other, God's action through the intervention of the Church, which is the forgiveness of sins" (CCC 1448).

"The Church, who through the bishop and his priests forgives sins in the name of Jesus Christ and determines the manner of satisfaction, also prays for the sinner and does penance with him. Thus, the sinner is healed and re-established in ecclesial communion" (1448).

PRAYER OF COVENANT UNION IN SACRAMENTAL LIFE:

Whenever we pray, we do so within the saving mystery of Christ's death and resurrection. In Baptism, we were buried into the death of Jesus. His blood on the cross has washed us clean. We have risen to new life, God's life, with our Risen Lord and Savior!

We meet Jesus, the Lamb of God who takes away the sins of the world, in the person of the priest in the Sacrament of Reconciliation. Through Holy Orders, the priest has become 'alter Christus (another Christ).' In confessing to him, I am confessing to Jesus. In receiving absolution, I am forgiven by Jesus through the priest.

In Confirmation, I received an Outpouring of the Holy Spirit. Through the sacraments of initiation, I have become the sanctuary of the Blessed Trinity. God abides in me, and I abide in God. I have been made holy because God who is holy dwells in me as His image and likeness!

EXERCISE NINE:
COVENANT UNION THROUGH THE LITURGY OF THE WORD
(REVELATION FIVE, WEEK ONE, DAY SEVEN, PAGE 167)
Do Lectio Divina with each paragraph
Session: 10-minute Duration

The Bible is God's Living Word. God speaks to us directly through human authorship. Using human authorship indicates God's commitment to being Emmanuel, our covenant God, living in our midst. He comes down to our level, to raise us to His!

In the beginning was the Word. The Word was with God. And the Word was God! The Word became flesh. He became one of us, to be able to die on our behalf. He became sin, so that we might share in God's righteousness. In His actions, Jesus demonstrated perfect covenant love.

Jesus is the Word made flesh. Jesus is the Good Shepherd and we are His flock. He laid down His life for us. No greater love does anyone have than to lay down one's life for one's friends. Jesus asks us to do the same.

The Liturgy of the Word is a proclamation. A proclamation engenders a crisis in the listener. It is a call to action. The proclaimed word of God acts as an urgent invitation to give ourselves to God in covenant union. It could also act to convict us because we have shut our ears to God's message of truth.

When Jesus speaks through the gospel account, He is addressing each one of us personally and as His covenant family. We are listening to Him in the here and now. He is here to bring us forgiveness of sin and transformation.

As our Savior and Lord, Jesus is asking that we encounter Him so that our lives will be transformed. The proclamation of the Gospel, therefore, makes Jesus' life present to us in a real and profound way.

When we have become familiar and open to the Word of God, both during the Liturgy and spiritual reading, Jesus' teachings become en-fleshed in us. We live, move, and have our being in Jesus' teachings. In doing so, we are re-created by the Holy Spirit. Jesus abides in us, and we in Him.

The Word of God always beckons us, patiently and persistently. *"Behold, I stand at the door and knock. If anyone hears my voice and opens the door, [then] I will enter his house and dine with him, and he with me. I will give the victor the right to sit with me on my throne, as I myself first won the victory and sit with my Father on his throne"* (Revelation 3: 20-21).

PRAYERS USING THE METHOD OF MEDITATION

This method of prayer has been in vogue since the middle ages. Saints Ignatius of Loyola and Teresa of Avila used the method themselves and taught it too.

Meditation always begins with a preparatory prayer. We ask God to direct all our intentions, desires, and actions, to the praise and service of God. The context of our relationship with God is set at the very beginning: during our prayer session, we are there on God's terms and we declare our earnest commitment to the Lord.

We then create the environment for our prayer session called the Composition of Place. We know the passage on which we will be praying. We can create whatever image we believe would help us to truly engage with the subject matter.

From looking at the passage, it becomes clear what grace or disposition we need in order to follow Jesus' teachings as expressed in the passage. So, we ask for that grace before we enter into the subject matter.

We then do a reflection on the passage. When done purposefully and with care, our reflection can stir our hearts deeply. Ignatius was adamant about tasting and relishing the truth in the passage. We will be moved to offer Jesus a response. It is important that we express directly to God in conversation the stirrings of our hearts engendered by the passage.

EXERCISE ONE:
CREATED IN GOD'S IMAGE AND LIKENESS

Genesis 1:27: *"God created mankind in his image; in the image of God he created them; male and female he created them."*

Preparatory Prayer: Prayer to the Holy Spirit.

Composition of Place: Imagine yourself in Paradise at the scene of man's creation as God's image and likeness

Grace: Ask to receive a true appreciation of your identity as God's image and likeness, being re-created by the Holy Spirit into the image of Jesus.

Reflection: God created only humans in His image and likeness. In doing so, God had a very definite purpose, to reveal to us the infinite depths of His divine love. He created us in His image and likeness so that He could share His divine life with us in covenant union. In desiring covenant union with us, God would share His divine life, offering us His love and everlasting commitment, holding nothing back, and in return, ask us to offer ourselves to Him, holding nothing back. The Garden of Eden symbolized this covenant union between God and His people. Covenant life required our wholehearted and selfless surrender to God. Why would the all-Perfect Being share all that He is with us, finite, imperfect, composite beings? Out of pure love, God gave us, composed of matter and spirit, the amazing capacity to share in the divine nature (2Peter 1:4), to become one with Him, to abide in Him and He in us.

Through sin, we rebelled against God and turned down this offer of covenant union with the Divine. However, God in His infinite goodness and love would not be deterred. God promised a Messiah to overthrow sin, and to establish God's reign among us: *"I will put enmity between you and the woman, and between your offspring and hers; they will strike at your head, while you strike at their heel"* (Genesis 3: 15). Through several covenants, God prepared His people for the coming of the Messiah. And this Messiah would be the Son of God, born of woman, and His name would be Jesus, God saves! Jesus then, on our behalf and in our stead, offered Himself as our perfect atonement on the cross. The Son of Man could become our Savior because He is Lord, the Son of God, and Second Person of the Blessed Trinity! Through His death and resurrection, Jesus established the Kingdom of God, permanently and irrevocably.

Through Jesus, God has entered into a new and everlasting covenant with us. We have been baptized into the death of Jesus and have risen with Him in His resurrection (Colossians 2: 12). Through our covenant union with God, we have entered the Kingdom of God. We belong to God as His sons and daughters! Through Jesus, the reign of darkness and evil has been overthrown. We gain entrance into the Kingdom of God by repenting of our sins, and acknowledging that we need salvation. We accept that Jesus alone can and will be our Savior and Lord!

Colloquy: Engage in a heartfelt conversation with the Blessed Trinity about your identity as God's image and likeness being perfected by the Holy Spirit into the image and likeness of Jesus.

EXERCISE TWO:
THE PROCLAMATION OF THE KINGDOM

Mark 1: 15: *"This is the time of fulfillment. The kingdom of God is at hand. Repent, and believe in the gospel."*

Preparatory Prayer: Prayer to the Holy Spirit.

Composition of Place: Imagine yourself by Lake Galilee as with many others you listen intently to Jesus proclaiming the arrival of the Kingdom of God through Him.

Grace: Ask for repentance and a deep faith to enter into God's Kingdom by accepting Jesus as your Lord and Savior!

Reflection: *This is the time of fulfillment:* The long wait for sinful and lost humanity has come to an end. Satan's domination over human hearts is over. A bright light, the Light of the world, is shining in our darkness. The Light is Jesus! *The Kingdom of God is at hand:* The reign of God, or being in covenant relationship with God, is here, in and through Jesus who is our Way, Truth, and Life. *Repent, and believe in the gospel:* Repentance, or *Metanoia* in Greek, is a 180-degree turnaround. We were turned away from God and were lost. Through repentance we turn towards God and accept His forgiveness and invitation to share in His own divine Life through His Son, Jesus Christ. The gospel is Good News that we have a Savior in Jesus Christ who is the Son of God. Jesus' teachings tell us who Jesus is and how He brings us into God's Trinitarian Life.

Colloquy: Engage in a heartfelt conversation of gratitude to Jesus for being your Savior and Lord and intercede for the grace of repentance and faith in Jesus.

EXERCISE THREE: WHO DO YOU SAY I AM?

Matthew 16: 15-17: *"He said to them, "But who do you say that I am?" Simon Peter said in reply, "You are the Messiah, the Son of the living God." Jesus said to him in reply, "Blessed are you, Simon son of Jonah. For flesh* *and blood has not revealed this to you, but my heavenly Father."*

Preparatory Prayer: Prayer to the Holy Spirit.

Composition of Place: Imagine yourself with Jesus in a deserted place so that without distraction, you can have a heart to heart conversation.

Grace: Ask that your commitment to Jesus as your Lord and Savior be wholehearted and generous.

Reflection: *You are the Messiah, the Son of the living God:* Jesus' divinity is slowly but surely being revealed to His disciples through the Holy Spirit. Peter's confession is very moving. He is in the presence of Jesus who is God as Moses was in the presence of God at the Burning Bush: our hearts understand what our minds can't comprehend. Peter's confession is a revelation beyond his competence! *Flesh and blood has not revealed this to you, but my heavenly Father:* No one is more invested in our return to God's Embrace through the sacrifice of Jesus, than His Heavenly Father. God has revealed to Peter who His Son is, a revelation that was beyond the competence of flesh and blood or a human source.

Colloquy: Respond to Jesus as He asks you to tell Him who He is for you. Is there anything that you desire from Him?

EXERCISE FOUR:
THE PARABLE OF THE PERSISTENT WIDOW

Luke 18: 1-8: *"Then he told them a parable about the necessity for them to pray always without becoming weary...And a widow in that town used to come to him and say, 'Render a just decision for me against my adversary. For a long time the judge was unwilling, but eventually he thought, 'While it is true that I neither fear God nor respect any human being, because this widow keeps bothering me I shall deliver a just decision for her lest she finally come and strike me.'" The Lord said, "Pay attention to what the dishonest judge says. Will not God then secure the rights of his chosen ones who call out to him day and night...But when the Son of Man comes, will he find faith on earth?"*

Preparatory Prayer: Prayer to the Holy Spirit

Composition of Place: Imagine yourself observing the persistent and persuasive widow convincing the unjust judge in his chambers.

Grace: Ask to increase your trust in God and perseverance in your prayer of petition.

Reflection: A parable is always making the case that while from the human perspective a solution is impossible, however, from God's perspective all things are possible. In Jesus' time, a widow had no rights as she received all her rights from her husband. Hence the prophets demanded that widows and orphans be treated with compassion and justice: *"Learn to do good. Make justice your aim: redress the wronged, hear the orphan's plea, defend the widow"* (Isaiah 1:17). In the parable, the widow has to deal with a judge *"who neither feared God nor respected any human being."* However, her persistence overcame his cynicism and indifference toward her. He even became afraid of the widow: *"I shall deliver a just decision for her lest she finally come and strike me."* The purpose of the parable is to emphasize the fact that we are *to pray always without becoming weary.* Perseverance in prayer highlights our seriousness of purpose as well as our willingness to trust God no matter what!

Colloquy: Have a conversation with the widow and listen to her advice about how you should carry yourself as a disciple of Jesus. And ask Jesus what He thinks of the widow's advice.

EXERCISE FIVE:
COME, ALL WHO LABOR AND ARE BURDENED
Matthew 11: 28-30: *"Come to me, all you who labor and are burdened, and I will give you rest. Take my yoke upon you and learn from me, for I am meek and humble of heart; and you will find rest for your selves. For my yoke is easy, and my burden light."*

Preparatory Prayer: Prayer to the Holy Spirit.

Composition of Place: Imagine yourself in the presence of Jesus who exudes compassion and love toward you who approach Him with sagging shoulders and drooping spirit.

Grace: To develop an abiding trust in the compassion and love that Jesus has for you.

Reflection: This passage has comforted and strengthened many disciples shouldering unbearable burdens. We are invited to approach Jesus with our burdens, presumably to be relieved of them. He asserts that He will refresh us by exchanging His yoke and burden for ours. He concludes with the notion that our souls will find rest in bearing His burden that is light and shouldering His yoke that is sweet. Jesus is referring to a two-oxen yoke. He presumably is the stronger and bigger ox, so to speak, and we are invited to be the other ox. Our burdens in life have become unbearable because we chose to haul them by ourselves. We quickly got exhausted and lost. However, when we allow Jesus to pull our burdens together with Him, they essentially become His. They are now lighter because Jesus is pulling with us. In having Him as our constant servant-companion, we can haul any load and bear any burden.

Colloquy: Jesus is listening to you as you unburden your soul and tell Him about your daily and long-standing difficulties and worries. He leaves you with His peace and assurance of His presence.

EXERCISE SIX: TREASURE IN HEAVEN

Matthew 6: 19-21: *"Do not store up for yourselves treasures on earth, where moth and decay destroy, and thieves break in and steal. But store up treasures in heaven, where neither moth nor decay destroys, nor thieves break in and steal. For where your treasure is, there also will your heart be."*

Preparatory Prayer: Prayer to the Holy Spirit.

Composition of Place: Imagine yourself in the presence of Jesus who exudes compassion and love toward you who approach Him with sagging shoulders and drooping spirit.

Grace: Ask for an increase of faith and wisdom to choose God over greed and money.

Reflection: Jesus is making it clear to us that no treasure on earth can ever satisfy us. Earthly treasure, of its very nature is passing, ephemeral, and therefore, can never satisfy us permanently: *"where moth and decay destroy, and thieves break in and steal."* Sin and our inordinate attachments are always trying to convince us that our ultimate happiness lies in earthly treasures. We have only to look around us and within us to know that such thinking leads to disappointment and turmoil of spirit. Jesus then corrects our biased and sinful world-view by telling us to *"store up treasures in heaven, where neither moth nor decay destroys, nor thieves break in and steal."* All along in His ministry, Jesus has been presenting Himself as our only true treasure, because He is the Way, Truth, and Life. In Jesus, we will be fully satisfied because we will be drinking from the source of Divine Life! We will experience covenant union with the Father through His Son, in the power of the Holy Spirit. To paraphrase Jesus, if Jesus is our treasure, then our hearts will always abide in true peace and joy. We will be in the Kingdom of God!

Colloquy: Have an honest conversation with Jesus about choosing between God and mammon. Tell Him of your struggle and listen to what He has to say.

EXERCISE SEVEN: THE LIGHT OF THE BODY

Matthew 6: 22-23: *"The lamp of the body is the eye. If your eye is sound, your whole body will be filled with light; but if your eye is bad, your whole body will be in darkness. And if the light in you is darkness, how great will the darkness be."*

Preparatory Prayer: Prayer to the Holy Spirit.

Composition of Place: After the crowds have left, you are alone with Jesus on the Mount of Beatitudes, in conversation about Him being the Light of the world and you reflecting His light.

Grace: Ask for the grace to reflect the light of Jesus through your witness that He is truly the Lord and Savior of the world.

Reflection: Jesus is the Light of the world. He came into our lives so that in His Presence, the darkness of our sin would be obliterated. There were those who accepted Jesus as their Messiah and Lord. Through Him they became children of the Light, and sons and daughters of the Living God! There were others, who rejected Jesus and God's plan of salvation for them. Those who have accepted Jesus have an eye that is sound. They have the Light of the world in them! Consequently, their whole lives are radiated by the Presence, joy, and light of the Risen Lord! Those who reject Jesus have an eye that is bad. Their lives are cast in shadow and darkness. And without Jesus in their lives to offer them forgiveness and bring them into the Father's embrace, their darkness will be great, indeed!

Colloquy: Have an honest conversation with Jesus about yourself: are you a child of the Light? Or are you more comfortable being in the twilight?

EXERCISE EIGHT: ANSWER TO PRAYER

Matthew 7: 7-8: *"Ask and it will be given to you; seek and you will find; knock and the door will be opened to you. For everyone who asks, receives; and the one who seeks, finds; and to the one who knocks, the door will be opened."*

Preparatory Prayer: Prayer to the Holy Spirit.

Composition of Place: Imagine yourself in the presence of Jesus, our Intercessor before His Father, who is listening intently to your prayer and is so eager to help.

Grace: Ask to constantly seek God's help without ever quitting.

Reflection: The Prayer of Petition or Intercession is essential to the disciple as we cannot save ourselves. Jesus is our Savior and Lord. Our intercession with Him puts this central reality front and center. In order for Jesus to be able to offer us forgiveness of our sins, and everlasting life in Him, we need to depend completely on Him, trusting Him in every circumstance of our lives. The literal translation of these verses from the Greek would read as follows: *ask and keep asking till it is given to you; similarly, seek and keep seeking and you will find...* There are two reasons why we need to persevere in our prayer: sometimes in the nitty-gritty of life, we get overwhelmed, and doubts about God set in. Through perseverance in prayer we reassert our faith in

Jesus as being greater than our circumstances and doubts, as always being our Emmanuel, God-with-us! Secondly, because of sin, we can be superficial and even dishonest with God, not really meaning what we say, or saying what we mean. Perseverance in prayer strengthens our commitment to having an honest and transparent relationship with God.

Colloquy: Have a conversation with Jesus about the quality of your trust and dependence on Him and how your prayer of petition can be improved.

EXERCISE NINE: THE TWO FOUNDATIONS

Matthew 7: 24; 26: *"Everyone who listens to these words of mine and acts on them will be like a wise man who built his house on rock... And everyone who listens to these words of mine but does not act on them will be like a fool who built his house on sand."*

Preparatory Prayer: Prayer to the Holy Spirit.

Composition of Place: After the crowds have left, you are alone with Jesus on the Mount of Beatitudes, in conversation about the foundation of your spiritual life.

Grace: Ask the Holy Spirit to strengthen the foundations of your discipleship.

Reflection: These are some of the last verses of the Sermon on the Mount, and act as a challenging re-cap of Jesus' teaching. Implicit in these verses is the all-important question that is staring us in the face: *Have you accepted Jesus as your Savior and Lord?* If you have, you will take His teachings very seriously. You will not pick and choose according to your whim and fancy. In accepting Jesus as your Savior and Lord, your life has changed. You are abiding in the peace and joy of the Risen Lord! Your house is built on rock. If, however, one does not act on the words of Jesus, then he is *"like a fool who built his house on sand."*

Colloquy: Talk to Jesus about what you need to strengthen your discipleship and listen to Him giving you the truth that will set you free.

EXERCISE TEN:
THE PARABLE OF THE WEEDS AMONG THE WHEAT
Matthew 13: 24-30: *"The kingdom of heaven may be likened to a man who sowed good seed in his field. While everyone was asleep his enemy came and sowed weeds all through the wheat, and then went off. When the crop grew and bore fruit, the weeds appeared as well... Let them grow together until harvest; then at harvest time I will say to the harvesters, "First collect the weeds and tie them in bundles for burning; but gather the wheat into my barn."*

Preparatory Prayer: Prayer to the Holy Spirit.

Composition of Place: Imagine yourself before a wheat field that is lush and without weeds. A month later you view the same scene and notice with much disappointment that it is infested with weeds.

Grace: Ask for an abiding trust in God's Providence, understanding that He who is within you is far greater than he who is without.

Reflection: This parable is peculiar to Matthew. It teaches us several valuable lessons. For one, our earthly pilgrimage will leave us with unanswered questions. We will wonder about the strong influence of evil in the world and in our own hearts and wish that God would use His power to overcome evil in a dramatic and convincing manner, once and for all. Yet, the parable tells us that the presence of evil will always be in our midst. While Jesus is victorious, and the war has been won, skirmishes between Satan and God will continue till the end of time. We need to trust the wisdom of God's ways, knowing that in Jesus we will overcome evil. Jesus made this point to Thomas: *"Blessed are those who have not seen and have believed"* (John 20: 29). Secondly, the householder who represents the Son of Man makes it very clear that in ministry and our dealings with others, it is important not to exclude anyone from God's merciful embrace. It is never our prerogative to judge and pass condemnation on others. That final judgment belongs exclusively to God. In this world, there will always be an admixture of good and evil. Our obligation is to practice patience and repentance and preach it through our words and actions.

Colloquy: Have an earnest conversation with Jesus regarding your difficulties with trusting Him in situations of confusion, disorder, and doubt. Listen to what He says.

PRAYERS USING IGNATIAN CONTEMPLATION

St. Ignatius of Loyola popularized the method of prayer that uses imagination as a major vehicle. He asks you to use your imagination in creating the Scriptural scene on which you are praying. You enter the scene as if you were in the audience that Jesus was addressing, or the individual that Jesus was healing.

Next, you consider, observe, and ponder what the persons are saying and doing, and then to reflect on yourself and draw some fruit from it.

Briefly, the method engages our imagination to better see God's mystery and to observe what is being said and done by Jesus. This method highlights the fact that our sense faculties are an integral part of our beings, and therefore, have to be an integral part of our relationship with God and our prayer.

Benefits from using Ignatian Contemplation: Ignatian contemplation is an affective method of prayer, engaging our whole being. It engages all the human faculties. What starts out as pure imagination, as one tries to engage God's mystery, ends up in imaginative faith.

Many who use this method will say quite categorically that they experienced God's Presence and

Mystery and were awed and subdued by it. For those who enjoy using the imagination in prayer, this method can be both restful and productive.

St. Ignatius seems to presume that this method could lead to a greatly simplified form of discursive prayer where God's presence and love is experienced with fewer words and thoughts, and more in silence and in the heart.

This method does not seem to work too well for those who have a logical and intellectual bent. Some have found to their relief and delight that when they stopped trying to paint God's Mystery on the canvas of their hearts, paradoxically, the images started to appear, and they could enter into God's Mystery through this method.

EXERCISE ONE:
REVIEWING WITH JESUS THE PAST TEN YEARS

Matthew 7: 21: *Not everyone who says to me, 'Lord, Lord,' will enter the kingdom of heaven, but only the one who does the will of my Father in heaven."*

Preparatory Prayer: Prayer to the Holy Spirit.

Composition of Place: It is the last day of your pilgrimage in the Holy Land. You have awakened before dawn and are seated on the shore of Lake Galilee. Jesus is present with you, along with Mary His mother, Peter,

114

John, and Mary Magdalene. In this intimate setting, you are doing an assessment of your discipleship over the past ten years.

Grace: Ask the Holy Spirit to derive much benefit from your communion with Jesus and His saints as you review the past ten years of your life.

Reflection: You have visited many of the holy sites in Galilee and Jerusalem. You are overwhelmed with gratitude and many other sentiments that you have not had time to put into words. This morning you have decided to begin an intimate conversation with Jesus about all that you have witnessed and what kind of bearing your pilgrimage is meant to have on your life. You are grateful and feel privileged that they are here to converse with you about the matters of your heart. In the course of the conversation, Jesus asks you to share about your journey in discipleship over the past ten years. They listen very attentively to your story. After you have finished, beginning with Jesus, they share their reflections. You listen attentively to each one of them. Then Jesus asks you what it is you would like from Him. What is your answer? Finally, Jesus tells you what it is He wants from you. The time has come for you to depart. You take your leave from Jesus and the others. Each one of them blesses you and offers you a special word to carry in your heart.

Colloquy: You go over the whole visit, interacting with Jesus and the others. You express your gratitude and other sentiments and feel deeply strengthened and ready to go home to live your discipleship more ardently and joyfully.

EXERCISE TWO:
WALKING THROUGH THE LAST DAYS OF YOUR LIFE

Mark 8:36: *"What profit is there for one to gain the whole world and forfeit his life?"*

Preparatory Prayer: Prayer to the Holy Spirit.

Composition of Place: After several visits with your doctor and tests, you are in his office waiting to listen to his assessment of your health. You are experiencing anxiety and uncertainty and your blood pressure has gone up as you await his arrival.

Grace: Ask the Holy Spirit to prepare you to die in peace and total acceptance of your life on earth and His will for you.

Reflection: You have decided to come alone to meet with your doctor. You've been able to convince your family that it is better for you to go alone. After your initial greetings, the doctor goes over the tests you have undergone. His conclusion at the end of his overview is that your cancer has spread into various organs through your lymph nodes and you have six months to live.

Chemotherapy would give you a few extra months, but your life is now dangling on a string, and you have six to nine months to live. Your doctor is very compassionate and you can sense his concern for you. However, he is also telling you the truth which only you can address. In your prayer you live the remaining days of your life going through the following steps:

1. You are all by yourself after you exit the doctor's office. You sit down on a bench in the park and try to get in touch with your feelings around your approaching death.

2. You come home and meet with your spouse and family. You tell them the news and the air in the room is charged with a multitude of feelings, their feelings toward you and yours toward them.

3. As the days go by and the sands in your glass keep ebbing, what are the loose ends you wish to tie, the unfinished business you want to address, the unhealed relationships that need forgiving and being forgiven?

4. You are praying on a daily basis. How would you describe your relationship with God? How would you assess your life as you have lived it? How would Jesus assess it?

5. You have a week to live, the last week on earth. What is it you wish to tell your spouse and family members? How would you like to be remembered?

How would you describe your last confession and sacrament of the sick?

6. You are in the last hour of life which is also your last hour before death and the beginning of eternal life. What are your sentiments and how are your loved ones around your bed supporting you?

Colloquy: You have a conversation with Jesus. You express your gratitude to Him for the forgiveness of your sins, for the gift of your Catholic faith, and for giving you the grace to accept His decision about your approaching death. You ask Jesus and Mary to take care of your family and to be with them as they journey through life. Finally, you ask that you approach your death with faith and trust in God's love and mercy.

EXERCISE THREE: JOSEPH BROUGHT TO PEACE

Matthew 1: 19-21: *"Joseph her husband, since he was a righteous man, yet unwilling to expose her to shame, decided to divorce her quietly. Such was his intention when, behold, the angel of the Lord appeared to him in a dream and said, "Joseph, son of David, do not be afraid to take Mary your wife into your home. For it is through the holy Spirit that this child has been conceived in her. She will bear a son and you are to name him Jesus, because he will save his people from their sins."*

Preparatory Prayer: Prayer to the Holy Spirit.

Composition of Place: Imagine you are present at the scene when the Archangel Gabriel appears to Joseph.

Grace: Ask the Holy Spirit to strengthen the foundations of your discipleship.

Reflection: *Joseph her husband, since he was a righteous man, yet unwilling to expose her to shame, decided to divorce her quietly:* Joseph is described as a righteous man whose life, therefore, was ordered according to the dictates of God's law. He saw Mary's pregnancy as a violation of God's righteousness, or the right order of things. But, instead of bringing her to a religious court of law, where the sentence would have been death by stoning (Deuteronomy 22: 20-21), he wanted to divorce her quietly. As Joseph's betrothed, Mary had the obligations of a wife to him. *Joseph, son of David, do not be afraid to take Mary your wife into your home. For it is through the holy Spirit that this child has been conceived in her:* The angel Gabriel lets Joseph in on God's plan of salvation, and that he had a significant role to play as the foster father of the Holy Family. So, it was in God's righteousness that Joseph take Mary to be his lawful wife. And Joseph was obedient. *She will bear a son and you are to name him Jesus, because he will save his people from their sins:* The angel Gabriel spells out more clearly God's plan of salvation to Joseph: His betrothed is pregnant, and will bear a son, and Joseph is to name him Jesus, which means *God saves,* as *"he will save his people from their sins!"*

Colloquy: Have a conversation with Joseph about how God made possible and brought immense good out of a situation that in his mind seemed impossible and rife with sin. Ask Jesus and Mary to strengthen your faith in God and obedience to His will.

EXERCISE FOUR: THE HEALING OF A PARALYTIC

Mark 2: 9-12: *"Which is easier, to say to the paralytic, 'Your sins are forgiven,' or to say, 'Rise, pick up your mat, and walk?' But that you may know that the Son of Man has authority to forgive sins on earth"* – he said to the paralytic, *"I say to you, rise, pick up your mat, and go home."* He rose, picked up his mat at once, and went away in the sight of everyone. They were all astounded and glorified God, saying, *"We have never seen anything like this" (Mark 2: 9-12).*

Preparatory Prayer: Prayer to the Holy Spirit.

Composition of Place: You are witnessing the amazing events that are unfolding in this crowded room of Peter's home in Capernaum.

Grace: Ask the Holy Spirit to strengthen your faith in Jesus, the Healer of your soul!

Reflection: *Your sins are forgiven:* Only God can forgive sin. If Jesus begins the encounter by first forgiving the paralytic his sins, then he is suggesting that he is God, and therefore also has the power to cure the man of his illness. *He rose, picked up his mat at once, and went away in the sight of everyone:* After Jesus forgives the man his sin, to the horrified disgust of his opponents he then heals the paralytic of his illness. The man's gesture of rising, picking up his mat, and walking away in the sight of everyone, is an indescribable sight to behold! *They were all astounded and glorified God, saying, "We have never seen anything like this:* God's actions in Creation and in healings make it very clear that God is incomprehensible to our minds, and totally other-than what we can ever imagine. The spontaneous response on our part, therefore, is astonishment, amazement, and gratitude and praise on our lips. As the crowd exclaimed, "We have never seen anything like this!"

Colloquy: Now that you have witnessed the miracle, what do you seek from Jesus and what advice does the healed man offer you?

EXERCISE FIVE:
JESUS HEALS THE BLIND DEMONIAC

Matthew 12: 22-24: *"Then they brought to him a demoniac who was blind and mute. He cured the mute person so that he could speak and see. All the crowd was astounded, and said, "Could this perhaps be the Son of David?" But when the Pharisees heard this, they said, "This man drives out demons only by the power of Beelzebul, the prince of demons."*

Preparatory Prayer: Prayer to the Holy Spirit.

Composition of Place: You are a witness to the miracle that takes place in the interaction between Jesus and the blind and mute demoniac.

Grace: Ask the Holy Spirit to strengthen your faith in Jesus, the Healer of your soul!

Reflection: Through this miracle, Jesus demonstrates that He is Messiah and Lord. He heals the blind and mute demoniac through His own power. Jesus demonstrates that He has come to overthrow the sway of Satan over people's lives. Only God can have such power over Beelzebul, the prince of demons. A good number of people have accepted Jesus as their Messiah. So they bring to Him the demoniac who was blind and mute. The miracle astounds them and leads them to ask a deeper question: *"Could this perhaps be the Son of David?"* They knew that the Messiah would spring from the seed of David and be king over the new and eternal kingdom. The Pharisees, on the other hand, are obstinately blinded to the truth. They are filled with hate to the point of making ridiculous assertions: *"this man drives out demons only by the power of Beelzebul, the prince of demons."* Besides pointing out the absurdity of the charge, Jesus asks them how they would interpret the work of Jewish exorcists (*your own people*). Blasphemy against the Holy Spirit is the sin of attributing to Satan what is the work of the Spirit of God: *"But if it is by the Spirit of God that I drive out demons, then the kingdom of God has come upon you"* (verse 28). While miracles are glimpses into the kingdom of God, they also display the power of sin over people who refuse to accept Jesus as Savior and Lord!

Colloquy: Now that you have witnessed the miracle, what do you seek from Jesus and what advice does the healed man offer you?

EXERCISE SIX:
THE WOMAN WITH A HEMORRHAGE

Mark 5: 30; 33-34: *"Jesus, aware at once that power had gone out from him, turned around in the crowd and asked, "Who has touched my clothes?" ... The woman, realizing what had happened to her, approached in fear and trembling. She fell down before Jesus and told him* the whole truth. He said to her, "Daughter, your faith has saved you. Go in peace and be cured of your affliction."

Preparatory Prayer: Prayer to the Holy Spirit.

Composition of Place: You are in the crowd being jostled as you witness the woman falling down before Jesus and being healed!

Grace: Ask for an intimate knowledge of our Lord who has become man for me, that I may love Him more and follow Him more closely.

Reflection: *She fell down before Jesus and told him the whole truth:* An important dimension of Jesus' healings is that either he touched the sick persons when healing them, or they touched him. This intimate contact between Jesus and the ones he saved suggests that He is Emmanuel, God among us, who is Son of God and son of man. In His presence, this woman who has been healed of her hemorrhage by touching Jesus, confessed the wonderful news of her healing even while she was afraid. *Daughter, your faith has saved you. Go in peace and be cured of your affliction:* Repeatedly, Jesus makes the point that the faith of the seeker heals him or her. In her recognition and acceptance of Jesus as Savior and Lord, the woman is healed of her affliction and saved because she has come into a new life through her relationship with Jesus.

Colloquy: Now that you have witnessed the miracle, what do you seek from Jesus and what advice does the healed woman offer you?

EXERCISE SEVEN:
THE CLEANSING OF THE SAMARITAN LEPER

Luke 17: 15-16; 19: *"And one of them, realizing he had been healed, returned, glorifying God in a loud voice; and he fell at the feet of Jesus and thanked him. He was a Samaritan... Then he said to him, "Stand up and go; your faith has saved you."*

Preparatory Prayer: Prayer to the Holy Spirit.

Composition of Place: You accompany the Samaritan leper when he realizes he has been healed and returns to Jesus. You witness the interaction between them.

Grace: Ask the Holy Spirit to be grateful like the Samaritan healed from his leprosy.

Reflection: *Realizing he had been healed, returned, glorifying God in a loud voice; and he fell at the feet of Jesus and thanked him. He was a Samaritan:* It must have taken the Samaritan leper great courage and trust to come to Jesus, along with the nine other Jewish lepers. As a Samaritan, he was considered an outcast. Jesus was a Jew. Would Jesus turn him down? Owing to his degrading sickness, his misery was great indeed! But even greater was his faith and trust in Jesus. His healing produced in him the authentic results of repentance or conversion: He returned to glorify God, and falling at the feet of Jesus, thanked him! *Then he (Jesus) said to him, "Stand up and go; your faith has saved you:* Jesus came to save us from our sin and offer us a share in God's divine life through Him. Having faith in Jesus, as the Samaritan did, is surrendering to Jesus as Savior and Lord. Jesus exercises His power within the context of faith, as He has come to bring us salvation from Satan, sin, and permanent death. His dismissal of the Samaritan is very moving: *"Stand up and go; your faith has saved you."*

Colloquy: Have a conversation with the Samaritan about his experience of salvation in Jesus. Then ask Jesus what it is He wants of you.

EXERCISE EIGHT: THE CRUCIFIXION

Prayer on John 19: 25-27: *"Standing by the cross of Jesus were his mother and his mother's sister, Mary the wife of Clopas, and Mary of Magdala. When Jesus saw his mother and the disciple there whom he loved, he said to his mother, "Woman, behold your son." Then he said to the disciple, "Behold, your mother." And from that hour the disciple took her into his home."*

Preparatory Prayer: Prayer to the Holy Spirit.

Composition of Place: You are present at the crucifixion of Jesus along with Mary, His mother, John, the beloved disciple, Mary Magdalene, and the other women.

Grace: Ask the Holy Spirit to reveal to you the depths of God's love revealed in the crucifixion and death of His Son on the cross.

Reflection: Only John tells us that Our Lady was present at her son's crucifixion and death. As a mother, Mary must have wondered about the rest of the disciples who abandoned Jesus. As a devout Jewess, she must have wondered how it was possible for the Jewish leadership to be so prejudiced against her son. Yet from her own experience of the human condition, as she experienced and observed it in her son's kenosis and her own, she must have had His disposition: *"Father, forgive them; they do not know what they are doing"* (Luke 23: 34). In this final act of love, before He surrendered His life to His Father, Jesus engages in an amazing act of covenant love and union. He bequeaths to His mother a special mission, in fact, the continuation of the same mission that was given to her at the Annunciation: to be the mother of His covenant family, with whom He has become one, and symbolized by John the beloved disciple. And in handing His mother to the safe-keeping of His beloved disciple, Jesus was asking His covenant family to always accord her a special place of honor and reverence in our hearts, similar to the honor and reverence Jesus always had for her. This has been the Church's understanding of the special connection between Mary, Mother of God, and God's Church, also known as God's covenant family.

Colloquy: In reverent silence at the mystery that has just unfolded, communicate with Mary, mother of Jesus, John the Beloved disciple, Mary Magdalene, Mary the wife of Clopas, Joseph of Arimathea and Nicodemus.

EXERCISE NINE:
JESUS APPEARS IN THE UPPER ROOM

John 20: 19-23: *"Jesus came and stood in their midst and said to them, "Peace be with you." When he had said this, he showed them his hands and his side. The disciples rejoiced when the saw the Lord. [Jesus] said to them again, "Peace be with you. As the Father has sent me, so I send you." And when he had said this, he breathed on them and said to them, "Receive the holy Spirit. Whose sins you forgive are forgiven them, and whole sins you retain are retained."*

Preparatory Prayer: Prayer to the Holy Spirit.

Composition of Place: You are present in the Upper Room with the disciples as the Risen Lord appears in your midst.

Grace: Ask the Holy Spirit to infuse you with the Risen Lord's peace and joy.

Reflection: In John, the Resurrection, Ascension, and Imparting of the Holy Spirit are seen as different aspects of the same divine mystery. The disciples are transformed by the gift of the Holy Spirit being given to them by the Risen Jesus. Two points are worthy of note in this resurrection event. Jesus, the Risen Lord, breathes the Holy Spirit into His apostles. He breathes into them His own divine life through His Holy Spirit. Secondly, through the Holy Spirit, Jesus gives His apostles the power to forgive and retain sin. God took an amazing risk, to allow humans to exercise this power in His name. Twenty centuries of chosen humans, our bishops and priests, exercising this power in Jesus' name, has turned out to be an immense grace. God always knows best.

As with Jesus, so with us, we will live and serve in the power and overshadowing of the Holy Spirit. This is what St. Cyril of Alexandria, circa 435, had to say about Genesis 2:7 *(the Lord God...blew into his nostrils the breath of life, and the man became a living being)* and John 20: 21-22: *"Christ's act (of redemption) was a renewal of that primal gift and of the inbreathing bestowed on us, bringing us back to the form of the initial holiness and carrying man's nature up, as a kind of first fruits among the holy apostles, into the holiness* bestowed on us initially at the first creation." The breathing of the Holy Spirit upon us by Jesus is our re-creation. We are begotten of the Spirit who will guide us to all truth and in doing so will give glory to Jesus!

Colloquy: Have a heart to heart conversation with the Risen Lord as He fills you with His peace and joy. What sentiments do you express to Him?

EXERCISE TEN:
THE OUTPOURING OF THE HOLY SPIRIT

Acts 2: 1-4: *"When the time for Pentecost was fulfilled, they were all in one place together. And suddenly there came from the sky a noise like a strong driving wind, and it filled the entire house in which they were. Then there appeared to them tongues as of fire, which parted and came to rest on each one of them. And they were all filled with the holy Spirit and began to speak in different tongues, as the Spirit enabled them to proclaim." [Please read Acts 2: 1-13 for a better appreciation of the passage].*

Preparatory Prayer: Prayer to the Holy Spirit.

Composition of Place: You are present in the Upper Room with the disciples as the Holy Spirit descends upon all of you and you know you are changed!

Grace: Ask the Holy Spirit to teach you how to live and act under His constant tutelage and power.

Reflection: The descent of the Holy Spirit upon the apostles reverberated with the power and majesty of God and brought about amazing transformation in the apostles and bystanders. The outpouring of the Holy Spirit occasioned the birth of the Church. The Holy Spirit is described as *"a strong driving wind,"* and *"tongues of fire."* Fire symbolized the presence of God to initiate the covenant on Sinai. Here the Holy Spirit acts upon the apostles, preparing them to proclaim the new covenant with its unique gift of the Divine Spirit. The apostles were filled with the Holy Spirit and began to express themselves in foreign tongues and make bold proclamations. The bystanders were utterly amazed and dumbfounded because they could understand the apostles speaking to them in their own tongues. What an amazing manifestation of God's power in and through the Holy Spirit!

Colloquy: Pour out your heart to the Holy Spirit in gratitude and adoration as He fills you with the peace and joy of the Risen Lord!

Made in the USA
Columbia, SC
03 September 2024

41598213R00072